THE
ULTIMATE
BASEBALL
TRIVIA
BOOK

THE ULTIMATE BASEBALL TRIVIA BOOK

by
Richard L. Vickroy
& Herbert A. Ruth

 Jonathan David Publishers, Inc.
Middle Village, New York 11379

To my mother, Anna,
who is very proud
of me

To my son, Joseph,
and to baseball

THE ULTIMATE
BASEBALL TRIVIA BOOK

Jonathan David Publishers, Inc.
68-22 Eliot Avenue
Middle Village, New York 11379

1989 1988 1987 1986
10 9 8 7 6 5 4 3 2 1

Library of Congress Cataloging-in-Publication Data
Vickroy, Richard L., 1961-
The ultimate baseball trivia book.

1. Baseball—United States—Miscellanea. I. Ruth, Herbert A.,
1926-   . II. Title.
GV867.3.V53   1986   796.357'093   85-29269

ISBN 0-8246-0311-7 (pbk.)

ISBN 0-8246-0329-X

Printed in the United States of America

CONTENTS

INTRODUCTION

This book contains many of the noteworthy—and dubious—achievements in the history of major league baseball. Unlike many trivia books, the answers in this book are not simply one or two words long. Wherever possible, information such as the date, opponent, and location is given to answer a question more completely.

This book is not just a steady diet of statistical firsts, lasts, and "onlies," but a healthy portion of the game's lighter side as well. Several chapters have questions regarding baseball's humorous vein. In addition, many sidelights of the grand old game are inserted between chapters.

You will find no disclaimer in this book separating records from before and during the "modern era," whenever that era supposedly started. Those records mentioned are products of the established National and American Leagues. All the information in this book is complete up to January 1, 1986.

Virtually all of the information has been researched and/or verified from periodicals and microfilm at the University of Pittsburgh at Johnstown and David A. Glosser Memorial libraries, as well as from authoritative baseball publications. Despite the wealth of information available to us and the many hours of research done, we are fallible creatures and so we apologize in advance for any mistakes or oversights that the reader notices.

The authors would like to acknowledge Rodger Kane, Donna Rafalski, and the many others whose efforts greatly expedited the publication of this work.

The contents of this book contain no fancy drawings or artwork of any sort. The art, we hope you find, is in the questions, answers, and sidelights themselves.

So fans, here's the beauty that was and is big league. If you're a fan, you've got stock in the corporation. Enjoy it!

Richard L. Vickroy
Herbert A. Ruth

1.

THE BATTER'S BOX

Questions

THE TOOLS OF IGNORANCE

1. *What catcher holds the record for number of games caught in a career?*

2. *Who was the first major league catcher to wear glasses?*

3. *What catcher caught four knuckleballers in one season?*

4. *What receiver caught the Niekro brothers' knuckleball act at Atlanta in 1973-74?*

5. *Who was the first left-handed catcher?*

6. *What catcher invented shin guards?*

7. *What catcher threw out the most runners attempting to steal in a game?*

8. *What catcher committed the most passed balls in one game?*

9. *What catcher nailed three would-be base stealers in a single inning?*

10. *What two catchers hold the record for most passed balls in one season?*

Answers

THE TOOLS OF IGNORANCE

1. Al Lopez, 1,918 games from 1928 to 1947.

2. Clint Courtney, NY Yankees, 1951.

3. Rick Ferrell, Washington, 1944. He caught knucklers Mickey Haefner, Roger Wolff, Johnny Niggeling, and Dutch Leonard.

4. Johnny Oates. He also caught 200-game winners Gaylord Perry, Luis Tiant, Tommy John, Jim Kaat, Steve Carlton, Don Sutton, and Jim Palmer.

5. William A. Harbridge, Hartford, 5/6/1876.

6. Roger Bresnahan, St. Louis Cardinals, 1907.

7. Charles "Duke" Farrell, Washington, threw out eight men on 5/11/1897.

8. Frank Gardner, Washington, let twelve go by on 5/10/1884.

9. Les Nunamaker, NY vs. Detroit, 8/3/14.

10. Charles Snyder had 99 for Boston in 1881. Michael Hines, also for Boston, let a like number go by in 1883.

Questions

11. *What catcher caught the most no-hit games?*

12. *Who invented the flap that protects the catcher's neck?*

13. *What three catchers caught in every game their teams played in one season?*

14. *What catcher holds the record for consecutive errorless games at that position?*

15. *Who holds the record for stolen bases by a catcher in one season?*

16. *What catcher holds the AL record for home runs in a season?*

Answers

11. Ray Schalk, 4, on 5/14/14, 5/31/14, 4/14/17, and 4/30/22.

12. Steve Yeager. Oddly enough, the reason behind it stemmed from a non-catching accident. In 1978, Yeager was kneeling in the on-deck circle when a bat from the hands of teammate Bill Russell splintered after hitting the ball. The broken bat flew back and hit Yeager in the throat, nearly severing his jugular vein.

13. Ray Mueller, Cincinnati, 1944
    Mike Tresh, Chicago White Sox, 1945
    Frankie Hayes, Philadelphia A's, 1944.

14. Yogi Berra, NY Yankees, 148 games. Berra handled 950 errorless chances from 7/28/57 through 5/10/59.

15. John Wathan stole 36 bases (caught 9 times) for Kansas City in 1982. He broke Ray Schalk's record of 30 set back in 1916.

16. Carlton Fisk hit 37 for the Chicago White Sox in 1985, including four as a designated hitter. Johnny Bench holds the major league mark with 45 for Cincinnati in 1970.

Questions

THE HIGH AND THE MIGHTY

17. Who is the only player to slam two home runs in the same inning twice?

18. Who struck the longest recorded home run?

19. Who is the only Hall of Famer to hit a fair ball out of Yankee Stadium?

20. What was the only team in major league history to have four players with 30 or more home runs in one season?

21. What team hit back-to-back home runs most often in one season?

22. Who holds the record for having homered in the most consecutive games?

23. Who holds the record for slugging the most homers in one week?

Answers

THE HIGH AND THE MIGHTY

17. Willie McCovey, 4/12/73 and 6/27/77.

18. Mickey Mantle, 4/17/53, in Griffith Stadium off Senator pitcher Chuck Stobbs. It traveled over the left field fence, 565 feet from home plate. Mantle, batting right-handed, blasted the ball against a beer sign 10 feet beyond the fence. It caromed across the street into a truck garden. However, signed affidavits presented to H. G. Salsinger of the *Detroit News* claim that Babe Ruth struck a home run at Briggs Stadium in 1926 that went 600 feet!

19. Josh Gibson, 1934, with the Pittsburgh Crawfords of the Negro leagues. It was hit over the triple deck, next to the bull pen in left field.

20. The 1977 Los Angeles Dodgers. Steve Garvey hit 33, Reggie Smith hit 32, Ron Cey hit 30, and Dusty Baker hit 30. It took Baker's blast on the last day of the season to accomplish this feat.

21. The Boston Red Sox did it 16 times in 1977.

22. Dale Long homered in 8 straight games with Pittsburgh in 1956.

23. Frank Howard hit 10 from 5/12/68 through 5/18/68.

Questions

24. *What two players share the record for grand slams in one season?*

25. *Who holds the record for home runs struck in one month?*

26. *Who is the only player to belt grand slams in consecutive games twice?*

27. *How many times did Mickey Mantle hit a home run from both sides of the plate in the same game?*

28. *What player, when ordered to bunt, blasted a game-winning homer in a World Series?*

29. *What player hit over 500 home runs in his career, yet never appeared in the World Series?*

30. *Who is the only player to belt home runs in his first two at bats in the big leagues?*

31. *What club struck the fewest home runs in a season?*

32. *Who hit the first National League home run?*

33. *Who was the first man to pound two grand slams in the same game?*

Answers

24. Ernie Banks, Chicago, 1955, and Jim Gentile, Baltimore, 1961. Each hit 5.

25. Rudy York hit 18 homers in the month of August, 1937, for Detroit.

26. Babe Ruth, 9/27/27 and 9/29/27, and again on 8/6/29 and 8/8/29.

27. Ten times.

28. Pittsburgh 1st baseman Bob Robertson missed a bunt sign and clubbed a three-run homer in the third game of the 1971 series against Baltimore, icing that win for the Pirates.

29. Ernie Banks.

30. Bob Nieman, St. Louis Browns, 9/14/51.

31. The 1908 Chicago White Sox hit the grand total of 3 home runs. Ed Walsh, Frank Isbell, and Fielder Jones did the lusty hitting.

32. Roscoe Barnes, Chicago, vs. Cincinnati, 5/2/1876.

33. Tony Lazzeri, NY Yankees, 5/24/36.

Questions

34. *What American League player hit that circuit's first grand slam?*

35. *What player holds the record for most home runs in the same park?*

36. *What was Roger Maris' batting average the year he hit 61 home runs?*

37. *What player has slammed home runs while playing left field, center field, right field, first base, and catcher in the same season?*

38. *What two sluggers have homered in more ballparks than anyone else?*

39. *Who was the only player to smash a ball over the double-deck left field bleachers at the Polo Grounds?*

40. *Who is the all-time left-handed home run hitter in the NL?*

41. *What "slugger" won the home run crown and not one of those hits left the park?*

42. *What two players share the season record for homers by a right-handed hitter?*

Answers

34. Herm McFarland, Chicago, 5/1/01.

35. Mel Ott, NY Giants, hit 323 homers in his home park, the Polo Grounds.

36. Maris hit .269 in 1961. The year Babe Ruth hit 60, his average was .356!

37. Johnny Bench, Cincinnati, 1970.

38. Frank Robinson and Rusty Staub, 32 different parks.

39. Philadelphia's Danny Litwhiler, off New York pitcher Ace Adams. Those bleachers were 505 feet away!

40. Willie McCovey, 521.

41. Tommy "The Wee" Leach, Pittsburgh, 1902. Leach won the home run crown with six inside-the-park blasts. It was the lowest number ever struck by a home run champ.

42. Jimmie Foxx, Philadelphia A's, 1932, and Hank Greenberg, Detroit, 1938, share the mark with 58 home runs.

Questions

43. Who holds the career record for grand slams?

44. What player hit the first home run under the lights?

45. Who was the first player to slam three homers in one game?

46. Who holds the record for homers as a leadoff batter in a single season?

47. What slugger hit the most home runs during the 1970s?

48. What player belted the first indoor homer?

49. Who are the four players to hit four consecutive homers in a game?

50. Who holds the record for inside-the-park home runs in one season?

51. What pitchers gave up Babe Ruth's last AL and NL home runs?

Answers

43. Lou Gehrig, 23.

44. Floyd "Babe" Herman, Brooklyn, at Cincinnati's Crosley Field, 7/10/35.

45. Ed Williamson, Chicago, 5/30/1884.

46. Bobby Bonds, San Francisco, 11 in 1973. He also holds the career record for leadoff homers with 35.

47. Willie Stargell, 296.

48. Mickey Mantle, in an exhibition game versus Houston in the Astrodome, 4/9/65.

49. Bob Lowe, Boston, 5/30/1894
    Lou Gehrig, New York (AL), 6/3/32
    Rocky Colavito, Cleveland, 6/10/59
    Mike Schmidt, Philadelphia, 4/17/76 (10 innings)
    Six other men have hit four homers in a game but not consecutively.

50. Hazen "Kiki"Cuyler, 8, Pittsburgh, 1925.

51. The AL pitcher was Washington's Sid Cohen on 9/29/34. The NL hurler who gave up Ruth's final homer was Pittsburgh's Guy Bush on 5/25/35.

Questions

52. *What pitchers gave up Hank Aaron's last NL and AL home runs?*

53. *Who was the only catcher to lead his league in home runs?*

54. *Who are the single season home run leaders at their respective positions (including DH)?*

55. *Who holds the NL record for home runs in one season?*

56. *What slugger has the most three-homer games to his credit?*

57. *What player led his league in home runs for seven straight seasons?*

58. *Who was the last man to lead the league in home runs while playing for a last-place team?*

59. *What Willie hit the first home run out of San Francisco's Candlestick Park?*

Answers

52. The NL pitcher was Cincinnati's Rawly Eastwick on 10/2/74. The AL hurler who surrendered Aaron's 755th and final homer was California's Dick Drago on 7/20/76.

53. Johnny Bench. He did it twice for Cincinnati. In 1970, Bench hit 45, and in 1972, 40.

54.

1B	Hank Greenberg	Detroit	58	1938
2B	Dave Johnson	Atlanta	43	1973
SS	Ernie Banks	Chicago (NL)	47	1958
3B	Mike Schmidt	Philadelphia	48	1980
OF	Roger Maris	New York (AL)	61	1961
OF	Babe Ruth	New York (AL)	60	1927
OF	Hack Wilson	Chicago (NL)	56	1930
C	Johnny Bench	Cincinnati	45	1970
P	Wes Ferrell	Cleveland	9	1931
DH	Greg Luzinski	Chicago (AL)	32	1983

55. Hack Wilson, Chicago, 56 in 1930.

56. Johnny Mize, 6.

57. Pittsburgh's Ralph Kiner paced the NL from 1946 through 1952 in homers.

58. Frank Howard led the AL with 44 homers while with the 10th-place Washington Senators in 1968.

59. Willie Kirkland, San Francisco, 4/13/60.

Questions

60. *What team holds the record for the most homers in a 162-game season?*

61. *What player holds the record for the most consecutive seasons with 20 or more homers?*

62. *Who was the first player to hit grand slams in consecutive innings?*

63. *What slugger did Babe Ruth surpass to become the all-time home run leader?*

64. *What is the greatest spread a home run leader has held over a runner-up in a season?*

65. *Who holds the NL record for home runs in a season by a left-handed hitter?*

Answers

60. The 1961 NY Yankees slugged 240. The 154-game season record is shared by the 1947 NY Giants and the 1956 Cincinnati Reds with 221.

61. Hank Aaron, 20, 1955 through 1974.

62. Jim Gentile, Baltimore, 5/9/61, in the 1st and 2nd innings. Jim Northrup of Detroit, 6/4/68, and Frank Robinson of Baltimore, 6/26/70, also did it.

63. The Babe surpassed Roger Connor in 1921. Connor hit all of his 137 homers in the 19th century.

64. Thirty-five home runs. Babe Ruth did it in 1920 (54 to 19) and again in 1921 (59 to 24).

65. Johnny Mize, NY Giants, 1947, 51.

Questions

FANNING THE BREEZE

66. *What player has the distinction of being the 3,000th strikeout victim of both Nolan Ryan and Bob Gibson?*

67. *What player appeared in the most consecutive games without striking out?*

68. *What player has struck out more often than anyone in major league history?*

69. *Who holds the record for the fewest strikeouts in a career of more than 2,000 at bats?*

70. *What batter struck out the most times in a single season?*

71. *What rookie struck out in his first at bat while sitting on the bench?*

72. *What player struck out the most consecutive times at the plate?*

Answers

FANNING THE BREEZE

66. Cesar Geronimo.

67. Joe Sewell, Cleveland. From 5/17/29 to 9/19/29 he appeared in 115 games and batted 437 times without fanning.

68. Reggie Jackson, 2,385, as of 1/1/86.

69. Joe Sewell struck out 114 times in 7,132 at bats. This is approximately once every 62 times at bat.

70. Bobby Bonds, San Francisco, 1970, whiffed 189 times in 663 at bats (157 games).

71. Dorian "Doe" Boyland. In a 1978 contest with Pittsburgh against the NY Mets, Boyland hurt his arm with the count 1 and 2 and left the game. Rennie Stennett replaced Boyland and promptly struck out. However, under the rules of scoring Boyland got the K.

72. Sandy Koufax struck out all 12 times he came to the plate in 1955 with Brooklyn. Chicago Cub Bill Hands struck out in 14 consecutive at bats in 1968, but he had one walk and two sacrifice hits in between.

Questions

THE HIT PARADE

73. Who holds the record for most RBIs in one game?

74. Who was the last player to bat .400?

75. Who won the most batting titles in his career?

76. What was the only team blessed with two .400 hitters in the same season?

77. Who recorded the highest single season batting average?

78. How many times did Babe Ruth win the batting crown?

Answers

THE HIT PARADE

73. "Sunny" Jim Bottomley, St. Louis Cardinals, 12 RBIs on 9/16/24.

74. Ted Williams hit .406 for the Red Sox in 1941. Bill Terry was the last National Leaguer to do so. He batted .401 for the 1930 NY Giants.

75. Ty Cobb, 12. Cobb won every year from 1907 through 1919 except for 1916 when he hit .371 to Tris Speaker's .386.

76. The 1894 Philadelphia Phillies. Right fielder Sam Thompson hit .404 and left fielder Ed Delahanty batted .400. The center fielder Billy Hamilton hit .399 while reserve outfielder Tuck Turner hit .416 in only 80 games. Third baseman Lave Cross hit .389 as the team compiled a league-leading .343. Where did such a fabulous hitting team finish? Fourth! 18 games behind Baltimore. Further, not one of these hitters won the batting crown. Hugh Duffy of Boston led the league with .438.

77. Hugh Duffy, Boston, hit .438 in 1894. Tip O'Neill blasted .442 for St. Louis in the old American Association in 1887, the year walks counted as hits.

78. Once.   .378 in 1924.

Questions

79. How many times did Ty Cobb win the home run title?

80. What player incredibly averaged .400 over a five-year span?

81. Who was the last NL player to lead the senior circuit in home runs and batting average in the same year?

82. What club holds the team record for total bases in one game?

83. Who was the first player to bat .300, steal 30 bases, and hit 30 homers in a season?

84. Who owns the highest lifetime batting average?

85. What player collected the most hits in one season?

86. Who is the only player to lead both leagues in homers, triples, and RBIs in a single season?

Answers

79. Once. In 1909, Cobb smacked 9 while winning the Triple Crown. In addition, Cobb batted .377 and knocked in 107 runs.

80. Rogers Hornsby, St. Louis Cardinals. From 1921 through 1925, Hornsby stroked 1,078 hits in 2,679 at bats for a .402 average.

81. Johnny Mize hit 28 homers and batted .349 for St. Louis in 1939.

82. Boston Red Sox, 60, vs. St. Louis, 6/8/50.

83. Ken Williams, St. Louis Browns, 1922. Despite this performance, teammate George Sisler was named the AL Player of the Year. Williams finished with a .332 average, 39 homers, and 37 stolen bases plus a league-leading 155 RBIs and scored 128 runs. However, Sisler's numbers were also impressive. He stroked 246 hits, belted 18 triples, scored 134 runs, logged a .420 batting average, and stole 51 bases, all league-leading statistics.

84. Ty Cobb, .367

85. George Sisler, 257, St. Louis Browns, 1920.

86. Jim Rice, Boston, 1978. He hit 46 homers, 15 triples, and had 139 RBIs.

Questions

87. *What player holds the record for triples in a single season?*

88. *Who are the only two players to win baseball's Triple Crown twice?*

89. *What is the only major league single season batting record that has never been bettered in the minors?*

90. *Who were the first and last players to win the Triple Crown?*

91. *Who was the last player to win a batting crown yet not hit a homer that year?*

92. *What club holds the record for runs scored in one season?*

93. *Talk about records that may never be broken! How many seasons did Ty Cobb hit .300 or better?*

94. *What former manager holds the record for sacrifice flies in a season?*

95. *Who are the only two players to hit for the cycle 3 times?*

Answers

87. J. Owen "Chief" Wilson, 36, Pittsburgh, 1912.

88. St. Louis' Rogers Hornsby (1922 and 1925) and Boston's Ted Williams (1942 and 1947).

89. The most triples hit in a season. This record belongs to Pittsburgh's J. Owen "Chief" Wilson with 36 in 1912. The closest player in the minors was Jack Cross. He hit 32 for London of the Michigan-Ontario League in 1925.

90. Hugh Duffy, 1894 Boston Braves, and Carl Yastrzemski, 1967 Boston Red Sox.

91. Rod Carew, Minnesota, 1972. Ginger Beaumont, Pittsburgh, 1911, and Zack Wheat, Brooklyn, 1918, were the only other men to do this.

92. The 1931 NY Yankees scored 1,067 runs, an average of 6.9 per game.

93. Twenty-three years in a row!

94. Gil Hodges hit 19 sacrifice flies for the Brooklyn Dodgers in 1954.

95. Babe Herman, Brooklyn, twice in 1931 and again in 1933. Bob Meusel did it for the Yankees in 1921, 1922, and 1928

Questions

96. *Who was the first player to acquire 3,000 hits and 500 home runs?*

97. *Who is the career leader in doubles?*

98. *What year and what players were involved in the largest point differential between batting champions?*

99. *Who is the all-time leader in triples?*

100. *Who recorded and what was the lowest average that won a batting crown?*

101. *What game produced the most total bases by both teams?*

102. *What is the record for most runs scored in one inning?*

103. *What four players have had 3,000 hits and 400 homers in their careers?*

104. *Who are the two 3,000 hit men to finish their careers with less than a .300 average?*

105. *When was the last time teammates finished first and second in a race for the batting title?*

Answers

96. Hank Aaron. He was followed by Willie Mays.

97. Tris Speaker hit 793 in his career with the Indians and the Red Sox.

98. Detroit's Ty Cobb hit .420 in 1911. National League batting king Honus Wagner of Pittsburgh hit .334. The difference between the two was 86 points.

99. Sam Crawford, 312.

100. Boston's Carl Yastrzemski won the AL batting crown in 1968 with a .301 average.

101. Philadelphia at Chicago, 5/17/79. The game, won by the Phillies 23-22 on Mike Schmidt's homer in the 10th, produced 97 total bases. There were 11 homers, 2 triples, 10 doubles, and 27 singles.

102. Chicago scored 18 runs in the 7th inning against Detroit on 9/6/1883.

103. Stan Musial, Hank Aaron, Willie Mays, and Carl Yastrzemski.

104. Al Kaline, .297, and Lou Brock, .293.

105. Don Mattingly (.343) and Dave Winfield (.340) of New York paced the AL in 1984. New York Giants Willie Mays (.345) and Don Mueller (.342) in 1954 were the last NL teammates to finish 1-2 in batting average.

Questions

106. What player racked up more 200-hit seasons than anyone else?

107. Who are the only five players to hit 20 doubles, 20 triples, and 20 home runs in the same season?

108. Who are the only two players to hit over 300 homers and steal over 300 bases?

109. What is the all-time team based on the highest single season batting averages at each position (including DH)?

110. What Pirate got six hits in a game against the Phillies and never hit the ball out of the infield?

111. Who was the only player to hit four triples in one game?

112. Who was the only player to amass over 400 total bases five times in his career?

Answers

106. Pete Rose, 10.

107.

Frank Schulte	1911	Chicago Cubs
Jim Bottomley	1928	St. Louis Cardinals
Jeff Heath	1941	Cleveland
Willie Mays	1957	New York Giants
George Brett	1979	Kansas City.

108. Willie Mays and Bobby Bonds.

109.

1B	George Sisler	1922	St. Louis Browns	.420
2B	Rogers Hornsby	1924	St. Louis Cardinals	.424
SS	Hughie Jennings	1897	Baltimore	.397
3B	George Brett	1980	Kansas City	.390
	John McGraw	1899	Baltimore	.390
LF	Joe Jackson	1911	Cleveland	.408
CF	Hugh Duffy	1894	Boston	.438
RF	Ty Cobb	1911	Detroit	.420
C	Bill Dickey	1936	New York Yankees	.362
P	Walter Johnson	1925	Washington	.433
DH	Hal McRae	1976	Kansas City	.332

110. Ginger Beaumont, 7/22/1899.

111. William Joyce, 5/18/1897, NY Giants.

112. Lou Gehrig.

Questions

113. *Who are the 16 members of the 3,000 hit club?*

114. *Who holds the record for most hits in an extra-inning game?*

115. *What two players share the record for most hits in a nine-inning game?*

116. *Who are the only two players to collect 200 or more hits in a season split between two teams?*

Answers

113.

Pete Rose	4,204
Ty Cobb	4,191
Hank Aaron	3,771
Stan Musial	3,630
Tris Speaker	3,515
Honus Wagner	3,430
Carl Yastrzemski	3,419
Eddie Collins	3,311
Willie Mays	3,283
Nap Lajoie	3,251
Paul Waner	3,152
Cap Anson	3,081
Rod Carew	3,053
Lou Brock	3,023
Al Kaline	3,007
Roberto Clemente	3,000

114. Johnny Burnett, Cleveland, rapped out 9 hits (7 singles, 2 doubles) in an 18-inning contest against Philadelphia, 7/10/32.

115. Wilbert Robinson, Baltimore, 6/10/1892, (6 singles, 1 double), and Rennie Stennett, Pittsburgh, 9/16/75, (4 singles, 2 doubles, 1 triple), jointly share the record of 7 hits in a 9-inning game. Both players' hits were consecutive.

116. Red Schoendienst, Milwaukee and the NY Giants, 1957, and Lou Brock, Chicago Cubs and St. Louis, 1964.

Questions

117. Only one catcher has ever led the league in triples. Who is he?

118. What player holds the record for singles in a season?

119. What player drove in the most runs in one season?

120. Who is the only player to hit four home runs in one game and three triples in another?

121. What two players appeared in over 150 games in a season without hitting into a double play?

122. Who are the only two catchers to win batting crowns?

123. What slugger holds the record for total bases in one game?

124. What player smacked the most doubles in a season?

125. Who were the two players to lead their leagues in batting while playing for two teams in one season?

Answers

117. Tim McCarver, St. Louis, 13, 1966.

118. Lloyd Waner, 198, in his rookie season with Pittsburgh in 1927.

119. Hack Wilson knocked in 190 runs for the 1930 Chicago Cubs. Lou Gehrig had 184 RBIs for the Yankees in 1931 to set the AL mark.

120. Willie Mays hit three triples on 9/15/60 and four homers on 4/30/61 for San Francisco.

121. Augie Galan with Chicago (NL) in 1935 and Dick McAuliffe for Detroit in 1968.

122. Cincinnati Reds Bubbles Hargrave (.353) in 1926 and Ernie Lombardi in 1938 (.342) and 1942 (.330). Lombardi's latter title was won as a member of the Boston Braves.

123. Milwaukee Braves' Joe Adcock, 18 (4 homers, 1 double), 7/31/54.

124. Earl Webb, 67, with the Boston Red Sox in 1931.

125. Dale Alexander hit .367 for Detroit and Boston in 1932 while Harry Walker copped the NL batting title in 1947 as a member of St. Louis and Philadelphia.

Questions

126. *Who holds the record for the most singles in a career?*

127. *Who was the only player to collect 250 hits in a season while playing for a cellar-dweller?*

128. *What player rapped the most extra-base hits in a season?*

129. *Who was the only utility man to win a batting title?*

130. *Who was the last man to win a batting title for a last-place team?*

131. *Who were the only two players in this century to hit .400 and fail to win the batting crown?*

132. *Who are the only two men to collect 3,000 hits yet fail to win a batting title?*

133. *What three players share the record for most runs scored in one inning?*

134. *What is the record for runs scored in one game by both clubs?*

Answers

126. Pete Rose, 3,173.

127. Chuck Klein, Philadelphia Phillies, 1930.

128. NY Yankee Babe Ruth hit 44 doubles, 16 triples, and 59 homers in 1921 for a total of 119 extra-base hits. The Bambino also collected 85 singles in pounding out an average of .378 and a slugging percentage of .846!

129. Billy Goodman, Boston Red Sox, 1950. He hit .354 while playing 45 games in the outfield, 27 at first, 21 at third, 5 at second, and 1 at shortstop.

130. Richie Ashburn hit .350 while playing for the Philadelphia Phils in 1958.

131. Joe Jackson, 1911 Cleveland, hit .408 and finished second to Ty Cobb's .420. Cobb, ironically, hit .401 in 1922 but lost the title to George Sisler's .420.

132. Eddie Collins and Lou Brock.

133. Tom Burns and Ed Williamson each scored thrice in the 7th inning for Chicago on 9/6/1883, while Boston's Sammy White scored three of the 17 runs that the Red Sox scored in the 7th inning on 6/18/53.

134. 49. Chicago Cubs over the Philadelphia Phillies, 26-23, 8/25/22.

Questions

135. *Who was the first member of the 3,000 hit club?*

136. *Who was the last .400 hitter to play for a first-place team?*

137. *Who is the only player to steal 30 bases and hit 30 homers five times?*

138. *Who are the only two men that have collected over 700 at bats in a season?*

139. *What was the only club to have five players with over 100 RBIs each in the same season?*

140. *What was the last team that had all three starting outfielders top the 100 RBI mark in the same season?*

Answers

135. Cap Anson.

136. Hughie Jennings, Baltimore, 1896.

137. Bobby Bonds.

138. Willie Wilson, 705, 1980 Kansas City, and Juan Samuel, 701, 1984 Philadelphia.

139. The 1936 New York Yankees. The club was led by Lou Gehrig with 152, followed by Joe DiMaggio with 125, Tony Lazzeri with 109, and Bill Dickey and George Selkirk with 107 each.

140. The 1984 Boston Red Sox. Center fielder Tony Armas had 123 RBIs, left fielder Jim Rice added 122, and right fielder Dwight Evans drove in 104.

Questions

IN A PINCH

141. *Who holds the record for the most consecutive pinch-hits?*

142. *What player struck the most pinch-hit home runs in his career?*

143. *Who collected the most pinch-hits in one season?*

144. *What club used the most pinch-runners in one inning?*

145. *Who holds the record for pinch-hit RBIs in a World Series?*

146. *Who was the first pinch-hitter to homer in the World Series?*

147. *Only two batsmen have blasted two pinch-hit home runs in a single World Series. Who are they?*

148. *Who are the only two pinch-hitters to hit two grand slams in a year?*

149. *Who was the only man to pinch-hit for Babe Ruth?*

150. *Who was the first designated hitter to blast a home run?*

Answers

IN A PINCH

141. Dave Philley of the Philadelphia Phillies stroked 9 consecutive pinch-hits. The first 8 were in September, 1958. The ninth hit came on 4/16/59.

142. Cliff Johnson, 19, as of 1/1/86.

143. Jose Morales, 25, Montreal, 1976.

144. The Chicago White Sox used 4 pinch-runners in the 9th inning of their game with Minnesota on 9/16/67. The Pale Hose ran Buddy Bradford, Tommie Agee, Bill Voss, and Rich Morales.

145. Dusty Rhodes, 6 RBIs in the four-game 1954 World Series against Cleveland.

146. Yogi Berra homered for the Yanks against Brooklyn on 10/2/47.

147. Chuck Essegian, Los Angeles, 1959, and Bernie Carbo, Boston, 1975.

148. Dave Johnson of Philadelphia and Mike Ivie of San Francisco, both in 1978.

149. George "Duffy" Lewis, Boston Red Sox.

150. Orlando Cepeda of the Boston Red Sox homered off NY Yankee reliever Sparky Lyle on 4/8/73.

Questions

151. What two players share the record for consecutive pinch-hit home runs?

152. Who was the only man to pinch-hit for Ted Williams?

153. Who was the first designated hitter in major league history?

154. Who was the only player to pinch-hit for Hank Aaron?

155. What pinch-hitter struck the most homers in one season?

156. Who was the only player to pinch-hit and pinch-run in the same game?

157. Who was the first DH to drive in 100 runs in a season?

Answers

151. Lee Lacy, Los Angeles, 1978, and Del Unser, Philadelphia, 1979, 3.

152. Carroll Hardy, 1960.

153. Ron Blomberg, New York, 4/5/73 against Boston. He walked on five pitches.

154. Mike Lum, 1969.

155. Johnny Frederick, 6, Brooklyn, 1932.

156. Pat Collins, St. Louis Browns, 6/8/23. In the 3rd inning of that game, the Browns' Homer Ezzell got on base safely only to discover that he had to go to the john. The Browns requested of Philadelphia A's manager Connie Mack to permit a courtesy runner. At that time the rules on courtesy runners were different from today. Mack okayed Collins to act as the courtesy runner knowing full well that Pat was very slow afoot. Ezzell felt fine at the end of the inning and returned to his position on the field. In the 9th inning, Collins was sent up to pinch-hit for pitcher Ray Kolp. He walked, and was no sooner on base when he was replaced by pinch-runner Cedric Durst.

157. Detroit's Rusty Staub, with 101 in 1977. Staub knocked in 121 the next year.

Questions

SPECIALISTS IN THE FIELD

158. What club holds the record for turning the most double plays in a season?

159. Who pulled off the first unassisted triple play?

160. When was the last time a triple play occurred without a ball being hit?

161. Who used the first hand protection or glove in the big leagues?

162. Who was the only center fielder to catch a foul fly ball?

163. What Hall of Fame 1st baseman fielded a grounder, threw to first, and caught it himself?

164. What outfielder threw three men out at first base in one game?

165. Who was the last player to win not only the Triple Crown but the fielding title that season as well?

Answers

SPECIALISTS IN THE FIELD

158. The 1949 Philadelphia Athletics turned 217 double plays.

159. Cleveland shortstop Neal Ball, 7/19/09.

160. Opening day of the season, 4/6/78. Houston pitcher Joe Sambito struck out Cincinnati batter Dan Driessen with Red teammates Joe Morgan at 3rd and George Foster at 1st. Foster tried to steal 2nd on the play but catcher Joe Ferguson threw to shortstop Roger Metzger at the base, trapping Foster between 1st and 2nd. Metzger then saw Morgan leaning too far from third and fired to 3rd baseman Enos Cabell. Cabell tagged out Morgan and immediately fired the ball back to Metzger who caught Foster trying to steal 2nd again. The Reds won anyway 11-9.

161. Charles C. Wait, 1875.

162. Johnny Mostil, Chicago White Sox, 1922.

163. George Sisler, alerted that his pitcher was not going to cover the bag, sped to catch his own throw and retire the batter at 1st.

164. Ty Cobb, playing right field for Detroit.

165. Joe "Ducky" Medwick, St. Louis Cardinals, 1937.

Questions

166. *What famous Cleveland Indian made two unassisted double plays in the same month while playing the* outfield?

167. *What infielder holds the record for consecutive games without committing an error?*

168. *What player took part in the most double plays in a single game?*

169. *Who was the only shortstop to play an entire doubleheader without a chance at that position?*

170. *Who are the only two men to capture the Triple Crown and lead their league in fielding?*

171. *What player has won the most fielding titles at different positions?*

172. *What outfielder started two triple plays in the same season?*

Answers

166. Center fielder Tris Speaker. "The Gray Eagle" often played very shallow and would double runners off 2nd after spearing line drives. The two double plays in April 1918 were part of the all-time record of 135 double plays for outfielders that Speaker holds. Three other outfielders pulled off two unassisted double plays in the same season but not in the same month.

167. Steve Garvey, San Diego 1st baseman had played from 6/26/83 to 4/15/85, 193 games, without a miscue.

168. Curt Blefary, Houston 1st baseman, 7, 5/4/69.

169. Toby Harrah, Texas, 6/26/76.

170. Rogers Hornsby, 2nd baseman for the 1922 Cardinals, and Joe Medwick, outfielder for the 1937 Cardinals.

171. Pete Rose has won fielding titles at 1st base (1980), 3rd base (1976), and in the outfield (1970-71, 1974).

172. Cleveland's Charlie Jamieson, 5/23/28 and 6/9/28.

Questions

173. What is the record for most errors in one game by both teams?

174. What outfielder was involved in the most double plays in a season?

175. Who is the only player to catch a 9-inning game and then start the second game of the doubleheader at shortstop?

Answers

173. 40, Boston (24) vs. St. Louis (16), 6/14/1876. The AL record is "only" 18, set by Chicago (12) and Detroit (6) on 5/6/03.

174. Oscar "Happy" Felsch, 15, Chicago White Sox, 1919.

175. Dave Roberts, Texas, 1980.

Questions

176. *Who were the last teammates to finish first and second in stolen bases in a season?*

177. *Who holds the single season mark for stolen bases?*

178. *What player stole home most often in his career?*

179. *What two men share the record for stealing home most often in a season?*

180. *Who was the first player to steal home twice in one game?*

181. *Who was the last player to steal home twice in one game?*

182. *What two players share the record of having stolen their way from first to home three times in their careers?*

183. *Who was the last player to steal his way from first to home in a game?*

184. *Who holds the record for consecutive stolen bases before being thrown out?*

Answers

TO CATCH A THIEF

176. Frank Taveras (70) and Omar Moreno (53), Pittsburgh, 1977.

177. Rickey Henderson, 130, Oakland, 1982.

178. Ty Cobb, 35 times.

179. Pete Reiser, Brooklyn, 1946, and Rod Carew, Minnesota, 1969, 7 times.

180. Joe Tinker, Chicago Cubs, 6/28/10.

181. Vic Power, Cleveland, 8/14/58.

182. Honus Wagner and Ty Cobb.

183. Dusty Baker, San Francisco, 6/27/84.

184. Davey Lopes stole 38 straight for Los Angeles in 1975. He was finally caught by Gary Carter of Montreal on 8/24/75 after having already stolen three bases in that game.

Questions

185. *What player was caught stealing most often in a season?*

186. *What two players share the record for stolen bases in one game?*

187. *What player stole home twice in World Series competition?*

188. *Who were the pitcher and catcher when Rickey Henderson broke Lou Brock's single season stolen base record?*

189. *Who stole the first base in baseball history?*

190. *What teammates hold the record for number of combined thefts in one season?*

191. *What leadoff hitter holds the record for having gone to bat the most times in one season without stealing a base?*

192. *What club holds the team record for most stolen bases in one season?*

Answers

185. Rickey Henderson, 42, Oakland, 1982, the same season he swiped a record 130.

186. George Gore, Chicago, 6/25/1881, and Billy Hamilton, Philadelphia, 8/31/1894. Each stole 7 bases.

187. Bob Meusel, NY Yankees, 10/6/21 and 10/7/28.

188. Milwaukee catcher Ted Simmons called for a pitchout from Brewer hurler Doc Medich with Rickey Henderson on 1st base in their game of 8/27/82. However, Henderson slid safely under shortstop Robin Yount's tag for stolen base #119, breaking the single-season mark of 118 set by Lou Brock in 1974. The third-inning heist was one of four that Henderson collected that night.

189. Ed Cuthbert, 7/28/1865.

190. Vince Coleman (110) and Willie McGee (56), St. Louis, 1985, totaled 166 stolen bases.

191. Pete Rose, Cincinnati, 1975. In over 750 plate appearances, Rose reached base safely over 300 times and never stole one base! He was caught once.

192. The 1893 NY Giants stole 426 bases in 136 games. The AL record is held by the 1976 Oakland A's with 341 stolen bases in 161 games.

Questions

193. What player has the highest successful stolen base percentage for one season (minimum 50 attempts)?

194. Who was the only player to lead both leagues in stolen bases?

195. What player participated in the most games without stealing a base?

196. What two players led their leagues in both homers and stolen bases in the same season?

197. What player set the record for most double plays grounded into in one season the same year he led the league in stolen bases!?

198. What man led his league in stolen bases for the most consecutive years?

199. What was the only team with three players over 50 stolen bases for one season?

200. Who is the only man to steal 70 or more bases for five consecutive years?

Answers

193. Max Carey stole 51 bases in 53 attempts (.962) for Pittsburgh in 1923.

194. Ron LeFlore stole 68 with Detroit (AL) in 1978 and 97 for Montreal (NL) in 1980.

195. Russ Nixon played in 906 games from 1957 to 1968. His twelve-year career saw him reach base safely over 825 times without ever stealing a base.

196. Ty Cobb hit 9 homers and stole 76 bases for Detroit in 1909. Chuck Klein also paced the league in those categories with 38 homers and 20 stolen bases with the Philadelphia Phillies in 1932.

197. Boston's Jackie Jensen grounded into a major league record 32 double plays in 1954, the same season he topped the AL in stolen bases with 22.

198. Luis Aparicio led the AL in steals for 9 years from 1956 through 1964.

199. The 1976 Oakland A's, with Bill North (75), Bert Campaneris (54), and Don Baylor (52).

200. Tim Raines, Montreal, 1981 through 1985.

Questions

DAD TAUGHT 'EM HOW

201. Pete Rose is the career hit leader for switch-hitters. What switch-hitter is second?

202. Who was the first switch-hitter to hit home runs from both sides of the plate in the same game?

203. Who are the only two AL switch-hitters to have 200 or more hits in a season?

204. Who is the only switch-hitter to collect 100 hits from each side of the plate in the same season?

205. Who are the only four switch-hitters to win batting titles?

206. What player homered from both sides of the plate in the same game most often?

207. Who are the only two switch-hitters to win the AL MVP?

208. Mickey Mantle is the career home run leader for switch-hitters with 536. What players are second and third respectively?

Answers

DAD TAUGHT 'EM HOW

201. Frankie Frisch, 2,880.

202. Augie Galan, Chicago Cubs, 6/25/37.

203. Buck Weaver pounded out 210 hits for the White Sox in 1920. Willie Wilson became the second switch-hitter to do so with Kansas City in 1980 with 230 hits.

204. Garry Templeton, St. Louis Cardinals, 1979.

205. Mickey Mantle, Pete Rose, Willie Wilson, and Willie McGee. Mantle won his only batting title for the Yankees in 1956 as part of the Triple Crown. Rose won titles in 1968, 1969, and 1973 for Cincinnati. Wilson won top honors for Kansas City in 1982 and McGee took the crown for St. Louis in 1985.

206. Mickey Mantle, 10.

207. New York's Mickey Mantle, in 1956, 1957, and 1962, and Oakland's Vida Blue in 1971. Blue, however, won the award based on his pitching performance.

208. Reggie Smith is second with 314 and Ted Simmons is third with 238.

Sidelights

FOR THE BATTER'S BOX

Tuba Catching

In the 1964 World Series, St. Louis reserve catcher Bob Uecker was catching baseballs in the outfield during warm-ups *with a tuba!*

The Lumber Companies

Here is the list of teams on which three players hit 30 or more home runs in the same season:

1929 Philadelphia	(NL)	Chuck Klein (43), Lefty O'Doul (32), Don Hurst (31)
1941 New York	(AL)	Charlie Keller (33), Tommy Henrich (31), Joe DiMaggio (30)
1947 New York	(AL)	Johnny Mize (51), Willard Marshall (36), Walker Cooper (35)
1950 Brooklyn	(NL)	Gil Hodges (32), Duke Snider (31), Roy Campanella (31)
1953 Brooklyn	(NL)	Duke Snider (42), Roy Campanella (41), Gil Hodges (31)

1956 Cincinnati	(NL)	Frank Robinson (38), Wally Post (36), Ted Kluszewski (35)
1959 Washington	(AL)	Harmon Killebrew (42), Jim Lemon (33), Bob Allison (30)
1961 Milwaukee	(NL)	Joe Adcock (35), Hank Aaron (34), Eddie Mathews (32)
1963 Minnesota	(AL)	Harmon Killebrew (45), Bob Allison (35), Jimmie Hall (33)
1963 San Francisco	(NL)	Willie McCovey (44), Willie Mays (38), Orlando Cepeda (34)
1964 Minnesota	(AL)	Harmon Killebrew (49), Bob Allison (32), Tony Oliva (32)
1964 San Francisco	(NL)	Willie Mays (47), Orlando Cepeda (31), Jim Ray Hart (31)
1965 Milwaukee	(NL)	Hank Aaron (32), Eddie Mathews (32), Mack Jones (31)
1966 San Francisco	(NL)	Willie Mays (37), Willie McCovey (36), Jim Ray Hart (33)
1966 Atlanta	(NL)	Hank Aaron (44), Joe Torre (36), Felipe Alou (31)
1970 Cincinnati	(NL)	Johnny Bench (45), Tony Perez (40), Lee May (34)
1973 Atlanta	(NL)	Dave Johnson (43), Darrell Evans (41), Hank Aaron (40)

| 1977 Boston | (AL) | Jim Rice (39), George Scott (33), Butch Hobson (30) |
| 1982 Milwaukee | (AL) | Gorman Thomas (39), Ben Oglivie (34), Cecil Cooper (32) |

Only one team has ever had *four* players who hit 30 or more homers in the same season. See question 20.

A Punch-and-Judy Hitter

In his 11-year career with 5 different clubs, utility infielder Mick Kelleher earned the distinction of having gone to bat most often without hitting a home run. From 1972 through 1982, Kelleher had 1,081 at bats and *zero* home runs.

Power and Speed

Here is the list of the six players who have hit 30 home runs and stolen 30 bases in the same season:

		HRs	SBs
Ken Williams	1922 St. Louis Browns	39 HRs	37 SBs
Willie Mays	1956 New York Giants	36	40
	1957 New York Giants	35	38
Hank Aaron	1963 Milwaukee Braves	44	31
Bobby Bonds	1969 San Francisco Giants	32	45
	1973 San Francisco Giants	39	43
	1975 New York Yankees	32	30
	1977 California Angels	37	41
	1978 Chicago White Sox/ Texas Rangers	31	43
Tommy Harper	1970 Milwaukee Brewers	31	38
Dale Murphy	1983 Atlanta Braves	36	30

No player has ever hit 40 home runs and stolen 40 bases in the same season.

Nerves of Steel

Here are the top ten pinch-hitters, listed according to the number of pinch-hits:

1.	Manny Mota	150
2.	Smokey Burgess	144
3.	Jose Morales	123
4.	Jerry Lynch	116
5.	Red Lucas	114
6.	Steve Braun	113
7.	Terry Crowley	108
8.	Gates Brown	107
9.	Mike Lum	103
10.	Rusty Staub	100

Gloves of Gold

Here is the list of the most Gold Glove Awards won by a player at each position:

Position	Player	No.
1B	George Scott	8
2B	Bill Mazeroski	8
3B	Brooks Robinson	16
SS	Mark Belanger	8
	Luis Aparicio	8
OF	Roberto Clemente	12
	Willie Mays	12
	Al Kaline	10
C	Johnny Bench	10
P	Jim Kaat	16

The Road Runners

The following players hold the single-season stolen base record for their clubs in that respective city:

National League

Atlanta Braves	Brett Butler	39	1983
Chicago Cubs	Bill Lange	100	1896
Cincinnati Reds	W. Arlie Latham	93	1891
Houston Astros	Cesar Cedeno	61	1977
Los Angeles Dodgers	Maury Wills	104	1962
Montreal Expos	Ron LeFlore	97	1980
New York Mets	Mookie Wilson	58	1982
Philadelphia Phillies	Billy Hamilton	115	1891
Pittsburgh Pirates	Omar Moreno	96	1980
San Diego Padres	Alan Wiggins	70	1984
San Francisco Giants	Bill North	58	1979
St. Louis Cardinals	Lou Brock	118	1974

American League

Baltimore Orioles	Luis Aparicio	57	1964
Boston Red Sox	Tommy Harper	54	1973
California Angels	Mickey Rivers	70	1975
Chicago White Sox	Rudy Law	77	1983
Cleveland Indians	Miguel Dilone	61	1980
Detroit Tigers	Ty Cobb	96	1915
Kansas City Royals	Willie Wilson	83	1979
Milwaukee Brewers	Paul Molitor	41	1982-83
Minnesota Twins	Rod Carew	49	1976
New York Yankees	Rickey Henderson	80	1985
Oakland A's	Rickey Henderson	130	1982
Seattle Mariners	Julio Cruz	59	1978
Texas Rangers	Bump Wills	52	1978
Toronto Blue Jays	Dave Collins	60	1984

Perfect Balance

St. Louis Cardinal Hall of Famer Stan Musial is fourth on the all-time hit list with 3,630. Of that total, Musial got exactly half of them (1,815) at home at Busch Stadium and half on the road!

2.

THE PITCHER'S MOUND

Questions

HITLESS WONDERS

209. *Who hurled the last perfect game in the majors?*

210. *Who was the only pitcher to throw back-to-back no-hitters?*

211. *Who threw the first no-hitter from the 60'-6" distance from the mound to home plate?*

212. *Who threw the first no-hitter against New York in Yankee Stadium?*

213. *What three batters broke up potential no-hitters by Tom Seaver in the ninth inning?*

214. *Who threw the only no-hitter in the morning?*

215. *Who threw the last no-hitter at Brooklyn's Ebbets Field?*

216. *Who was the first pitcher to lose a game after hurling nine hitless innings?*

217. *What five pitchers have thrown two no-hitters in the same season?*

Answers

HITLESS WONDERS

209. Mike Witt, California, at Texas, 9/30/84. The Angels won 1-0 on the last day of the season.

210. Johnny Vander Meer, Cincinnati. He no-hit the Boston Bees on 6/11/38, 3-0. His second no-hitter was on 6/15/38, a 5-0 classic against the Brooklyn Dodgers. The latter ruined the Bums' first night game ever and sent 38,748 Flatbush faithful home in a daze. Vander Meer's string of hitless innings ended at 21 2/3 on 6/19/38, when Boston's Debs Garms opened the fourth inning with a single.

211. William Hawke, Baltimore, vs. Washington, 8/16/1893.

212. Bob Feller, Cleveland, 4/30/46. He claimed this was his greatest thrill in baseball.

213. Jimmy Qualls, Cubs, Leron Lee, Padres, and Joe Wallis, Cubs. Seaver finally pitched his first no-hitter on 6/16/78, against St. Louis.

214. George "Hooks" Wiltse, NY Giants, vs. Philadelphia, 7/4/08.

215. Sal Maglie, a 5-0 win over Philadelphia, 9/25/56.

216. Earl Moore, Cleveland, vs. Chicago, 5/9/01. He lost the game in the 10th inning on two hits.

217.
Johnny Vander Meer	Cincinnati	1938
Allie Reynolds	New York Yankees	1951
Virgil Trucks	Detroit	1952
Jim Maloney	Cincinnati	1965
Nolan Ryan	California	1973

Questions

218. *What rookie pitched a no-hitter in his first start and never completed another game?*

219. *Who was the only pitcher to throw a no-hitter in his first game?*

220. *Gaylord Perry threw his only no-hitter on 9/17/68 against St. Louis while with San Francisco. The next day the Cardinals' pitcher turned the tables and no-hit the Giants. Who was that St. Louis pitcher?*

221. *Who were the pitchers involved in a nine-inning game which saw only one hit?*

222. *Who hurled the first perfect game in the big leagues?*

223. *What four pitchers combined for a no-hitter in 1975?*

224. *What pitcher recorded the only opening-day no-hitter?*

225. *Who is the only pitcher to hurl five no-hitters?*

226. *Who were the pinch-hitter, catcher, and home plate umpire involved in the final out of Don Larsen's perfect game in the 1956 World Series?*

227. *Who hit the fly ball caught by center fielder Harry Craft that put the lid on Johnny Vander Meer's second straight no-hitter?*

Answers

218. Bobo Holloman, St. Louis Browns, vs. Philadelphia, 5/6/53. He was 29 when he came up.

219. Charles Jones, Cincinnati, 10/15/1892.

220. Ray Washburn.

221. Sandy Koufax pitched a perfect game, 1-0 win over Chicago on 9/9/65. The Cubs' Bob Hendley surrendered just one Dodger hit, a two-out double by Lou Johnson in the seventh inning.

222. John Lee Richmond, Worcester over Providence, 6/11/1880.

223. Oakland A's Vida Blue (5 innings), Glenn Abbott (1), Paul Lindblad (1), and Rollie Fingers (2) combined to no-hit California 5-0, 9/28/75.

224. Cleveland's Bob Feller no-hit Chicago 1-0 on 4/16/40.

225. Nolan Ryan.

226. Dale Mitchell took, Yogi Berra caught, and Babe Pinelli called strike three, Monday, October 8, 1956, at Yankee Stadium. It was also Pinelli's last game as a home plate umpire.

227. Leo Durocher.

Questions

"...AND BATTING NINTH"

228. *What pitcher ended his career with a total of 58 pinch hits?*

229. *What pitcher hit the most home runs in one season?*

230. *What pitcher holds the single season batting average record for that position?*

231. *What pitcher homered in his first at bat and tripled in his second at bat, then played for 21 more years in the big leagues and never hit another homer?*

232. *Who was the only pitcher to lead the majors in home runs?*

Answers

"...AND BATTING NINTH"

228. Charles "Red" Ruffing, 1924-47.

229. Wes Ferrell, Cleveland, hit 9 homers in 1931. He also holds the career homer record for a pitcher with 38.

230. The great Walter Johnson hit .433 in 97 at bats for Washington in 1925.

231. Hoyt Wilhelm.

232. Babe Ruth, Boston Red Sox, 1918. The Sultan of Swat struck 11.

Questions

233. Who was the last American League pitcher to hit a homer before the advent of the designated hitter (DH) rule?

234. Who was the last pitcher to hit an inside-the-park grand slam?

235. Who is the only pitcher to hit two grand slams in a single game?

236. Who is the only pitcher to hit three home runs in a single game?

237. What pitcher had the most .300 seasons at the plate?

238. Who was the last AL pitcher to get a hit before the DH rule was adopted?

Answers

233. Roric Harrison, Baltimore, 10/3/72, off Cleveland's Ray Lamb.

234. Mel Stottlemyre, NY vs. Boston, 7/20/65.

235. Tony Cloninger, Atlanta, 7/3/66. With his clouts off San Francisco pitchers Bob Priddy in the 1st and Ray Sadecki in the 4th, Cloninger became the only National Leaguer to accomplish that feat. He also set the RBI record for pitchers in that game with 9.

236. Jim Tobin, Boston Braves, 5/13/42.

237. Red Ruffing, 8.

238. New York's Larry Gowell laced a 3rd-inning double off Milwaukee's Jim Lonborg on 10/4/72. It was his only at bat in the majors.

Questions

NOBODY HOME

239. *What pitcher hurled the longest string of shut-out innings?*

240. *Who was the only pitcher to hurl two shutouts in one day?*

241. *Who holds the record for career 1-0 wins?*

242. *What was the longest scoreless game in the big leagues?*

243. *What two pitchers share the record for shut-outs in one season?*

244. *What pitcher tossed the most shutouts in his career?*

245. *What is the record for hits in a game by a team that was shut out?*

Answers

NOBODY HOME

239. Don Drysdale of the Los Angeles Dodgers hurled 58²/₃ consecutive scoreless innings in 1968. The Phil's Howie Bedell ended the string with a sacrifice fly on 6/8/68.

240. Ed Reulbach, 9/26/08. Both games went nine innings and resulted in 5-0 and 3-0 wins for Chicago over Brooklyn.

241. Walter Johnson, 38.

242. The Houston Astros and the New York Mets played 23 scoreless innings on 4/15/68. Houston scored in the bottom of the 24th inning to win 1-0.

243. George Bradley, St. Louis, 1876, and Grover Cleveland Alexander, Philadelphia, 1916, share the record of 16.

244. Walter Johnson, 113.

245. The New York Giants garnered 14 hits when they were shut out by Chicago's Larry Cheney on 9/14/13. The Cleveland Indians tied the mark when Milt Gaston of Washington blanked them on 7/10/28.

Questions

246. What is the record for the most runs scored by a team that shut out its opponent?

247. Who pitched the most 1-0 wins in a single season?

248. What pitcher lost 14 shutout games in a single season?

Answers

246. Providence beat Philadelphia 28-0 on 8/21/1883.

247. The mark is jointly held by Leslie "Bullet Joe" Bush (1918), Ewell Russell (1913), Walter Johnson (1913, 1919), Carl Hubbell (1933), and Dean Chance (1964). Each had five 1-0 wins in a season.

248. James Devlin, Louisville, 1876. He won 30 and lost 35 that season.

Questions

THE ROSIN BAG

249. *What pitcher won the most games in a season?*

250. *What pitcher won a record nine ERA titles in his career?*

251. *What pitcher hurled the most consecutive hitless innings?*

252. *What pitcher holds the lifetime record for losses in the majors?*

253. *What two pitchers share the record for wins without a loss at the start of the season in the American League?*

254. *What pitcher served up Roberto Clemente's 3,000th and final hit?*

255. *What pitcher threw both left-handed and right-handed?*

256. *What frustrated relief pitcher gave up 29 hits and yet still won the game?*

257. *What pitcher retired the most consecutive batters?*

Answers

THE ROSIN BAG

249. Charles "Old Hoss" Radbourn was 60-12 for Providence in 1884 with a 1.45 ERA. The AL record is held by Jack Chesbro who was 41-12 with New York in 1904.

250. Lefty Grove.

251. Cy Young, 24⅓ with the Boston Red Sox in 1904.

252. Cy Young, 313. It just so happens he also won the most games ever, too, 511.

253. Johnny Allen was 15-0 with Cleveland in 1937. Dave McNally duplicated that mark with 1969 Baltimore.

254. Jon Matlack, NY Mets, 9/30/72. The hit was a 4th-inning double in Pittsburgh.

255. Tony Mullane, 1881-94. He had 31 career shutouts and an ERA of 3.46. He holds the dubious distinction of facing a record 22 batters in an inning, 6/18/1894. For the most part, Mullane threw right-handed.

256. Ed Rommel, Philadelphia A's, 7/10/32. His team prevailed over Cleveland, 18-17.

257. Jim Barr, San Francisco, 41. He retired the last 21 Pirates on 8/23/72 and the first 20 Cardinals on 8/29/72.

Questions

258. *What pitcher owns the lowest ERA for a single season?*

259. *Who was the only pitcher to lead the league in winning percentage, strikeouts, and ERA in the same year more than once?*

260. *What Hall of Famer was known for his "Fog Ball"?*

261. *What Hall of Famer threw the "Fadeaway Ball"?*

262. *Who was famous for his "Flutterball"?*

263. *What hurler called his pitch the "Bat Dodger"?*

264. *What hurler won a game without throwing a pitch to the batter?*

265. *What right-hander had the most victories in the American League?*

266. *What pitcher committed the most balks in one season?*

267. *Who has been clocked as baseball's fastest pitcher?*

Answers

258. Dutch Leonard of the 1914 Red Sox had an ERA of 1.01 in 233 innings. Ferdie Schupp of the 1916 Giants fell 14 innings shy of qualifying for the record but his 0.90 ERA is a remarkable feat nonetheless.

259. Robert Moses "Lefty" Grove, Philadelphia A's. Not only was he the lone pitcher to do it 3 times, but he did it in successive years as well, 1929-31.

260. Dizzy Dean. It put the batters "into a fog."

261. Christy Mathewson. It has come to be known as the screwball.

262. Hoyt Wilhelm, the knuckleballer.

263. Leroy "Satchel" Paige.

264. Nick Altrock, Chicago (AL), 1906. Reliever Altrock picked the lead runner off 3rd base in the top of the ninth. The White Sox scored the winning run in the bottom of the inning.

265. Walter Johnson, 416.

266. Steve Carlton, Philadelphia, 11 in 1979.

267. Nolan Ryan's "Express" was clocked at 100.9 miles per hour in 1974.

Questions

268. Only 18 pitchers have won 300 games in their careers. Who are they?

269. Who was the only pitcher to lead the league in *wins* and *losses* in the same season?

270. Who is the winningest black or Latin pitcher of all-time?

271. What major league staff had the fewest complete games in a season?

272. Who was the first pitcher to win an ERA title for a last-place team?

Answers

268.

Cy Young	511
Walter Johnson	416
Christy Mathewson	374
Grover C. Alexander	373
Warren Spahn	363
Kid Nichols	361
Jim "Pud" Galvin	361
Tim Keefe	341
John Clarkson	327
Eddie Plank	325
Gaylord Perry	314
Steve Carlton	314
Mickey Welch	309
Charles Radbourn	308
Tom Seaver	304
Lefty Grove	300
Phil Niekro	300
Early Wynn	300.

269. Phil Niekro went 21-21 with Atlanta in 1979. He shared his victory title with his brother Joe of Houston!

270. Ferguson Jenkins, 284.

271. The 1977 San Diego Padres managed only 6 complete games. Bob Owchinko led the team with 3. Bob Shirley, Dave Freisleben, and Randy Jones had the others.

272. Bob Friend, 1955 Pittsburgh, led the NL with a 2.84 ERA.

Questions

273. What pitching great went six straight seasons with an ERA under 2.00?

274. What pitcher hurled the most consecutive innings in the same season without giving up a home run?

275. What reliever has the record for the longest stretch of innings without giving up a gopher ball?

276. Who threw the outlawed "Puff Ball"?

277. Who was the last pitcher to hurl consecutive 30-win seasons?

278. Who threw his "Eephus" pitch to Ted Williams in the 1946 All-Star Game?

279. Who holds the record for the highest winning percentage in one season (minimum 16 decisions)?

280. What pitcher lost the most games in a season?

Answers

273. Grover Cleveland "Pete" Alexander, 1915 through 1920.

274. Allan Sothoron, 178 innings, 1921, while pitching for the AL St. Louis Browns, Boston Red Sox, and Cleveland Indians.

275. Dale Murray, 247⅓ innings from 1974 through 1977, with Montreal and Cincinnati.

276. Gaylord Perry. While with the Atlanta Braves in 1981, he was forbidden to saturate the ball with rosin. The pitch would give off a puff of powder appearance when released. The ruling came from NL president Chub Feeney.

277. Grover Cleveland Alexander, Philadelphia Phillies, 1916-17, a total of 63 wins.

278. Pittsburgh's Truett "Rip" Sewell. Terrible Ted hit it out of the park.

279. Pittsburgh's Roy Face went 18-1 for a percentage of .947 in 1959.

280. John Coleman, 48 losses (11 wins) in 1883 with Philadelphia.

Questions

281. What pitcher surrendered the most hits in one year?

282. What pitcher led the majors in losses one year and wins the next year?

283. What two 200-game winners finished their careers with a winning percentage under .500?

284. What pitcher tossed the most one-hitters?

285. What pitcher recorded the highest ERA to lead the league?

286. Who was the first pitcher to win over 350 games?

287. Who is accused of throwing the "Dirt Ball"?

288. What pitcher started the most consecutive games without a relief appearance?

289. What pitcher holds the record for most opening day starts?

Answers

281. John Coleman gave up 809 hits in 548 innings with Philly in 1883. The AL mark is held by Baltimore's Joe McGinnity who allowed 412 hits in 382 innings in 1901.

282. Ed Rommel of the Philadelphia A's led the league in losses with 23 in 1921 and paced the AL in wins the next season with 27.

283. Bobo Newsom, 211-222 (.487), and Jack Powell, 248-255 (.493).

284. Bob Feller, 11.

285. Early Wynn, Cleveland, 3.20 ERA in 1950 paced the AL. Bill Walker of the Giants led the NL with a 3.08 ERA in 1929.

286. Pud Galvin, 361, at the end of a career that stretched from 1879 to 1892.

287. Ferguson Jenkins. By pushing dirt into the seams, Jenkins was said to have the same effect on a ball as a spitter.

288. Steve Carlton, 512.

289. Tom Seaver, 16.

Questions

THE FEELING OF RELIEF

290. *What pitcher made the most relief appearances in his career?*

291. *What two men share the mark for most saves in a season?*

292. *Who was the first major league pitcher hired solely as a reliever?*

293. *What reliever retired Stan Musial 49 times in a row?*

294. *What reliever won the most games in his career?*

295. *What pitcher holds the record for consecutive relief appearances without a start?*

296. *What pitcher appeared most often in one season?*

Answers

THE FEELING OF RELIEF

290. Hoyt Wilhelm, 1,018, 1952-72.

291. Dan Quisenberry, Kansas City, 1983, and Bruce Sutter, St. Louis, 1984, each saved 45 games.

292. Otey Crandall, NY Giants, 1908-18. Doc later hurled for St. Louis (NL) and Boston (NL), and spent two years in the Federal League in between. He compiled 25 career saves.

293. Clem Labine.

294. Hoyt Wilhelm.

295. Sparky Lyle, 899 consecutive games in relief from 1967 to 1982. Lyle never started a game.

296. Mike Marshall appeared in 106 games for Los Angeles in 1974. Marshall also holds the AL record with 90 for Minnesota in 1979.

Questions

297. *What reliever has recorded the most saves?*

298. *What pitcher chalked up the most relief wins in one season?*

299. *What club used the most relief pitchers in a 9-inning game?*

300. *Who was the only man to win an ERA title pitching strictly in relief?*

Answers

297. Rollie Fingers, 341.

298. Roy Face won 18 games in relief for Pittsburgh in 1959.

299. The St. Louis Browns used 8 relievers against Chicago on 10/2/49. The club's reasoning behind this was for the fans to see each of the staff's nine pitchers for one inning in that season finale.

300. Hoyt Wilhelm, 2.43 ERA with the NY Giants in 1952, his rookie season.

Questions

K

301. Who holds the record for striking out ten or more batters in a game?

302. Who holds the record for strikeouts in three consecutive games?

303. What pitcher struck out the most consecutive batters?

304. Who holds the record for consecutive seasons with 200 or more strikeouts?

305. What four pitchers share the record of 19 strikeouts in a 9-inning game?

306. What two pitchers share the record for strikeouts in their first game?

307. What pitcher holds the record for consecutive strikeout titles?

308. Who were the first teammates to finish 1-2 in strikeouts in the same year?

Answers

K

301. Nolan Ryan, 158, as of 1/1/86.

302. Nolan, Ryan, 47 in 27$^1/_3$ innings, 8/12/74 through 8/20/74 for California.

303. Tom Seaver, NY Mets, struck out ten consecutive San Diego Padres on 4/22/70.

304. Tom Seaver, 9, 1968-76.

305.

Charles Sweeney	Providence	6/7/1884
Steve Carlton	St. Louis	9/15/1969
Tom Seaver	NY Mets	4/22/1970
Nolan Ryan	California	8/12/1974.

306. Karl Spooner, Brooklyn, 9/22/54, and J. R. Richard, Houston, 9/5/71, each had 15.

307. Walter Johnson, 8, 1912-19.

308. Los Angeles hurlers Don Drysdale (232) and Sandy Koufax (216) in 1962. The only other time this was accomplished was in 1976 when California aces Nolan Ryan (327) and Frank Tanana (261) topped the AL.

Questions

309. What pitcher struck out the most batters in one season?

310. What hurler fanned the most consecutive batters to start his career?

311. What pitcher holds the AL mark for strikeouts?

312. What pitcher has fanned the most batters in a career?

313. What pitcher fanned 19 batters in a game and still lost?

314. What pitcher holds the NL record for most strikeouts by a right-hander in a season?

315. What pitcher struck out the most batters in an extra-inning game?

316. Who was the first pitcher to break Walter Johnson's strikeout record?

317. What pitcher holds the record for most strikeouts by a left-hander in a season?

Answers

309. Nolan Ryan, 383, California, 1973. Ryan's record topped the old mark of Sandy Koufax by one, set in 1965. However, Ryan accomplished his feat in ten fewer innings pitched and despite never facing an opposing pitcher because of the designated hitter rule.

310. Sammy Stewart fanned the first seven Chicago batters he faced in his big league debut with Baltimore, 9/1/78.

311. Walter Johnson, 3,506.

312. Nolan Ryan, 4,083, as of 1/1/86.

313. Steve Carlton, St. Louis, vs. New York, 9/15/69. Mets' outfielder Ron Swoboda's two homers beat the Cards 4-3.

314. J. R. Richard, 313, Houston, 1979.

315. Tom Cheney fanned 21 Orioles in a 16-inning game for Washington, 9/12/62.

316. Nolan Ryan broke the 55-year-old record first. Brad Mills of the Montreal Expos was caught looking for career strikeout 3,507 on 4/27/83 at Montreal. Steve Carlton in turn moved ahead of Ryan on 6/7/83 when he K'd St. Louis batter Lonnie Smith at Veterans Stadium. Ryan has since regained the lead.

317. Rube Waddell, 349, Philadelphia, 1904.

Questions

20/20

318. What pitcher had the most 20-win seasons?

319. Who holds the highest winning percentage in a single season for pitchers winning 20 or more games?

320. What was the team with four 20-game winners that lost the World Series?

321. Who are the only three pitchers that won 20 games at age 20?

322. Who was the only Puerto Rican to win 20 games in a season?

323. Who are the only two pitchers to win 20 games twice after age 40?

324. Who are the four pitchers who won 20 or more games in their first full season and returned to win 20 later in their careers?

325. Baltimore has had twenty-three 20-game winners over the years, and twenty-one of them played under Earl Weaver. Who were the two pitchers that did not?

Answers

20/20

318. Cy Young, 16. Fourteen of those years were consecutive, 1891-1904! Also in 1907-08.

319. Ron Guidry, NY Yankees, went 25-3 in 1978 for an amazing .893 percentage.

320. The 1971 Baltimore Orioles. The Pittsburgh Pirates won the series 4-3. In doing so, the Bucs defeated a staff that included Jim Palmer (20-9), Dave McNally (21-5), Mike Cuellar (20-9), and Pat Dobson (20-8).

321. Christy Mathewson, NY Giants, was the first to turn the trick in 1901. Bob Feller did it with Cleveland in 1939, and Dwight Gooden became the third to do so in 1985 with the NY Mets.

322. Ed Figueroa, NY Yankees, 1978.

323. Cy Young and Warren Spahn.

324. Wes Ferrell, Larry Jansen, Boo Ferriss, and Vida Blue.

325. Steve Barber won 20 games under manager Billy Hitchcock in 1963 while Mike Boddicker won 20 for skipper Joe Altobelli in 1984.

Questions

326. What AL team had four 20-game winners yet failed to win the pennant?

327. Who was the last pitcher to win 20 games for the Washington Senators?

328. What 20-game winner had the highest ERA?

329. Who is the only career 200-game winner never to have won 20 in a season?

330. Who was the last pitcher to win 20 games one year and lose 20 the next?

331. Who was the last pitcher to lose 20 games one year and win 20 the next?

332. Who was the only 20-game loser to appear in the World Series?

333. What pitcher was the last to win 20 games in his rookie season?

334. What Hall of Famer had ten straight 20-loss seasons?

Answers

326. The 1920 Chicago White Sox, despite pitchers Red Faber (23-13), Lefty Williams (22-14), Dickie Kerr (21-9), and Eddie Cicotte (21-10), finished two games behind the pennant-winning Cleveland Indians.

327. Bob Porterfield was 22-10 in 1953 including 9 shutouts. Of his total of 87 wins in the big leagues, *23* were shutouts!

328. Louis "Bobo" Newsom. In 1938, Newsom went 20-16 for the St. Louis Browns with the whopping ERA of 5.07!

329. Milt Pappas went 209-154 from 1957 to 1973 without ever winning 20 in a season.

330. Steve Carlton was 27-10 for Philadelphia in 1972 and went 13-20 for them in 1973.

331. Randy Jones rebounded from 8-22 in 1974 to 20-12 in 1975 for San Diego.

332. George Mullin of the 1907 Detroit Tigers was 20-20 during the season and promptly lost two more games to the Cubs in the World Series.

333. Tom Browning was 20-9 for Cincinnati in 1985.

334. James "Pud" Galvin, 1879-88. He managed to wind up his 14-year career with a record of 365-309.

Sidelights

FOR THE PITCHER'S MOUND

Perfect in a Pinch

Babe Ruth must have been in a cranky mood that day, June 23, 1917. The Bambino was furious when plate umpire Clarence "Brick" Owens awarded a walk to Washington's first batter, Ray Morgan. For his temper tantrum, Ruth was promptly thrown out of the game. Ernie Shore was summoned from the bull pen immediately. He had no time to warm up. However, Morgan was caught stealing. Shore then faced 26 batters and not one reached base. Yes, Ernie Shore's performance is classified in the Hall of Fame as a perfect game, even though he was not the starting pitcher!

Always Good for a Laugh

Lefty Gomez was not called "Goofy" for nothing. The first time Gomez batted against fireballer Bob Feller, he repeatedly struck matches and threw them across home plate. The umpire inquired, "What the hell are you doing?" Lefty told the arbitrator, "I just want to make sure Feller can see me."

Later in his life, after open-heart surgery that involved a triple bypass, Gomez was heard to say, "That's the first triple I ever got in my life."

Three in One

The following are the eight men who executed unassisted triple plays in major league history:

Neal Ball	Cleveland SS	7/19/09
Bill Wambsganss	Cleveland 2B	10/10/20 (World Series)
George Burns	Boston (AL) 1B	9/14/23
Ernest Padgett	Boston (NL) SS	10/06/23
Glenn Wright	Pittsburgh SS	5/07/25
Jimmy Cooney	Chicago (NL) SS	5/30/27
Johnny Neun	Detroit 1B	5/31/27
Ron Hansen	Washington SS	7/30/68

A Rose by Any Other Name

Today in baseball they are commonly called the slider, the palm ball, the fork ball, the changeup, etc. In the earlier days of the game they were called the upshoot, the outshoot, the drop, and the horseshoe curve. All eras of the game have had the fastball and the knuckleball.

True to His Name

On July 7, 1978, while taking wind sprints in the Baltimore outfield, Texas pitcher Doc Medich heard the call, "Is there a doctor in the house?" Medich, who specialized in orthopedic medicine during the off-season, raced to the scene. Behind the Oriole dugout, Germain Languth was having a coronary. Medich applied cardio-pulmonary resuscitation until paramedics could reach the scene. That was one save on the diamond that the box scores did not record!

A Psychological Pitch

During a game in 1981, Gaylord Perry, often suspected of throwing a spitball, rolled a baseball from the Atlanta dugout toward base umpire Eric Gregg. Gregg stooped to pick up the ball, and it slipped out of his hands. Perry had loaded it with petroleum jelly!

Big Winners, Big Losers

Winning 20 games is no small task for a pitcher. On the other hand, not too many pitchers are kept in the starting rotation long enough to lose 20 in a season. To both win and lose 20 games in a season is even more unlikely, given the advent of four- and five-man starting rotations at the turn of the century. Here are the names of the eight pitchers who did just that, however, and their respective records:

Bill Dineen	21-21	1902	Boston (AL)
Joe McGinnity	31-20	1903	New York (NL)
Irv Young	20-21	1905	Boston (NL)
George Mullin	20-20	1907	Detroit (AL)
Jim Scott	20-20	1913	Chicago (AL)
Walter Johnson	25-20	1916	Washington (AL)
Wilbur Wood	24-20	1973	Chicago (AL)
Phil Niekro	21-20	1979	Atlanta (NL)

3.

THE ANNUAL SHOWCASE

The Midsummer Classic   (335-389)
The Fall Classic   (390-484)
Sidelights

Questions

THE MIDSUMMER CLASSIC

335. Who is the only man to play five different positions in the All-Star Game?

336. Who is the youngest player to appear in an All-Star Game?

337. What player has the highest lifetime batting average in All-Star Games?

338. Who originated the All-Star Game?

339. What five "Jones boys" have appeared in the All-Star Game?

340. Who is the oldest player to appear in the All-Star Game?

341. Who threw the first pitch in All-Star play?

342. Who were the four men to lead off the All-Star Game with home runs?

Answers

THE MIDSUMMER CLASSIC

335. Pete Rose played 2nd base, left field, right field, 3rd base, and 1st base in that order.

336. Dwight Gooden, New York Mets pitcher, was 19 years, 7 months, 24 days old on 7/10/84.

337. Charley Gehringer, Detroit, was 10 for 20 in 5 games for a .500 average.

338. *Chicago Tribune* sportswriter Arch Ward.

339.

	National League
Willie	1950 Phillies
Sam	1955 Cubs and 1959 Giants
Cleon	1969 Mets
Randy	1975-76 Padres
	American League
Ruppert	1977 Mariners.

340. Leroy "Satchel" Paige, 7/14/53, at the age of 47 years, 7 days.

341. Vernon "Lefty" Gomez. He considered it his greatest thrill in baseball. In the original contest, Gomez also drove in the game's first run for the AL.

342.

Frankie Frisch	St. Louis (NL)	1934
Lou Boudreau	Cleveland (AL)	1942
Willie Mays	San Francisco (NL)	1965
Joe Morgan	Cincinnati (NL)	1977.

Questions

343. What AL All-Star smacked a line drive off Dizzy Dean's foot that hastened the end of Dean's career?

344. What two players share the record for hitting safely in seven straight All-Star Games?

345. Who is the only player to belt two triples in an All-Star Game?

346. What All-Star Game had the largest attendance?

347. When was the first night All-Star Game played and what strange strategy was employed by the AL manager?

348. Who are the only two players to reach base safely five times in an All-Star Game?

349. What All-Star Game saw the first appearance of black players?

Answers

343. Earl Averill, Cleveland (AL), 7/7/37.

344. Mickey Mantle and Joe Morgan.

345. Rod Carew, Minnesota (AL), 7/11/78. Both 1st and 3rd inning triples came off Vida Blue of San Francisco (NL).

346. The 1981 midsummer classic in Cleveland's Municipal Stadium was played before 72,086 fans. The game officially ended the 50-day players' strike of that season.

347. 1943, Shibe Park, Philadelphia. The game was won by the AL 5-3. Joe McCarthy had six of his Yankees on his roster but did not play a single one. The reason? "Marse Joe" dashed the gossip that he had padded his lineup with his own players.

348. Phil Cavaretta, Chicago (NL), had a triple, single, and three walks in the 1944 game. This mark was equalled in the 1946 contest by Ted Williams. The "Thumper" had 2 homers, 2 singles, and a walk.

349. The 1949 game, played in Ebbets Field and won by the AL 11-7. The first black players were Jackie Robinson, Roy Campanella, and Don Newcombe, all of Brooklyn, and Larry Doby of the Cleveland Indians.

Questions

350. What was the first All-Star Game to go extra innings?

351. What All-Star Game had the most players from the same team voted to the starting lineup?

352. What All-Star Game had no extra-base hits?

353. When was the first indoor All-Star Game?

354. What pitcher has struck out the most batters in All-Star play?

355. What is the All-Star Game's Most Valuable Player award titled?

356. Who was the pitcher literally blown off the mound in the 1961 All-Star Game?

357. Who are the two players to win the All-Star MVP award twice?

Answers

350. The 1950 game at Comiskey Park, Chicago. It went 14 innings and was won by the NL 4-3.

351. The 1957 game in Busch Stadium, St. Louis, won by the AL 6-5. Every regular from the Cincinnati Reds was selected except George Crowe. Commissioner Ford Frick ordered Gus Bell and Wally Post dropped from the roster. Manager Walter Alston later restored Bell to the squad. All-Star voting by the fans was subsequently dropped until 1970.

352. The 1958 game at Memorial Stadium, Baltimore, won by the AL 4-3, produced only 13 singles.

353. 1968, in the Houston Astrodome, won by the NL. The 1-0 contest was also the lowest scoring game in All-Star history.

354. Don Drysdale, 19.

355. The Arch Ward Trophy. It was named in honor of the *Chicago Tribune* sportswriter who originated the game in 1933.

356. Stu Miller, San Francisco (NL), first game, at Candlestick Park. Because there was a man on base, Miller was charged with a balk!

357. Los Angeles Dodger Steve Garvey, 1974 and 1978, and Montreal Expo Gary Carter, 1981 and 1984.

Questions

358. What six pitchers appeared in the first All-Star Game back in 1933?

359. Who is the only pitcher to win an All-Star Game without retiring a batter?

360. What player has the most RBIs in All-Star competition?

361. What outfielder set the record for assists in the All-Star Game by throwing two runners out at home plate?

362. Who is the youngest pitcher to win the All-Star Game?

363. Who was the first player to hit two homers in an All-Star Game?

364. Who were the last two St. Louis Browns chosen for the midsummer classic?

Answers

358. AL manager Connie Mack used Lefty Gomez (Yankees), Alvin Crowder (Senators), and Lefty Grove (A's). NL skipper John McGraw used Will Bill Hallahan (Cards), Lon Warneke (Cubs), and Carl Hubbell (Giants). McGraw came out of retirement to manage that first All-Star Game.

359. Dean Stone, Washington (AL), 7/13/54. Stone caught Red Schoendienst stealing home to finish the NL 8th. The AL scored the winning runs in the bottom of that inning to give Stone credit for the victory.

360. Ted Williams, 12.

361. Dave Parker, Pittsburgh (NL), 1979. His two throws helped preserve a 7-6 NL victory and earned him the game's MVP.

362. Jerry Walker of Baltimore (AL) won the second All-Star Game of 1959 at the age of 20.

363. Arky Vaughan, Pittsburgh (NL), 1941. Since then it has been accomplished by Ted Williams in 1946, Al Rosen in 1954, and Willie McCovey in 1969.

364. Pitcher Satchel Paige and shortstop Billy Hunter in the 1953 contest.

Questions

365. Who was the first New York Met to appear in the All-Star Game?

366. Who has struck out the most times in All-Star play?

367. Who is the only pitcher to serve up three gopher balls in one All-Star Game?

368. Who is the only pitcher to start an All-Star Game for each league?

369. Who was the first player to appear for both leagues in the All-Star Game?

370. Who was the first All-Star to get four hits in one classic?

371. Who is the only player to steal home in an All-Star Game?

372. What player holds the All-Star record for home runs?

373. Who is the only All-Star to hit a homer and steal a base in the same game?

374. What two fielders pulled off unassisted double plays in the All-Star Game?

Answers

365. Richie Ashburn, second game of 1962.

366. Mickey Mantle, 17.

367. Jim Palmer, Baltimore (AL), 7/19/77.

368. Vida Blue. He started the 1971 game with Oakland (AL) and the 1978 game with San Francisco (NL).

369. Leonard "Schoolboy" Rowe, Detroit (AL), 1936, and Philadelphia (NL), 1947.

370. Joe "Ducky" Medwick, 7/7/37, St. Louis (NL).

371. Pie Traynor, 7/10/34, Pittsburgh (NL).

372. Stan Musial, 6.

373. Willie Mays, San Francisco (NL), second game in 1960.

374. First baseman Pete Runnels, Boston (AL), second game in 1959, and Lee May, Houston (NL), 1972.

Questions

375. Who was the only Seattle Pilot chosen for the All-Star Game?

376. Who are the only two Mexicans to appear in the All-Star Game?

377. What two players share the record for most RBIs in an All-Star Game?

378. What five NL pitchers combined for the first All-Star shutout?

379. What player homered to end the longest All-Star Game?

380. What was the only year an All-Star Game was not played since its inception?

381. What happened to the $100,999.39 in gate receipts from the 1944 All-Star Game?

Answers

375. Mike Hegan, 1969. He was replaced by his teammate Don Mincher for the game.

376. Bobby Avila, Cleveland (AL), 1952, 1954-55, and Fernando Valenzuela, Los Angeles (NL), 1981-85.

377. Ted Williams, 1946, and Al Rosen, 1954, share the mark with five.

378. Paul Derringer, Bucky Walters, Whitlow Wyatt, Larry French, and Carl Hubbell combined for a 4-0 whitewash of the AL in the 1940 game at Sportsman's Park, St. Louis. The first AL shutout occurred in 1946 at Boston's Fenway Park. The 12-0 win was pitched by Bob Feller, Hal Newhouser, and Jack Kramer.

379. Cincinnati's Tony Perez homered off Oakland's Jim Hunter to give the NL a 2-1, 15-inning triumph over the AL in the 1967 game at Anaheim Stadium.

380. The 1945 contest was cancelled because of wartime travel restrictions.

381. It went to buy baseball equipment for the armed forces.

Questions

382. What was the first year in which two All-Star Games were played?

383. When was the All-Star Game first played in a new stadium?

384. What manager lost the most All-Star Games?

385. What family has had the most sons in the All-Star Game?

386. What catcher threw out the most would-be base stealers in an All-Star Game?

387. Who hit the only All-Star grand slam?

388. Who is the only player to start consecutive All-Star Games for different leagues?

389. What pitcher was the victim of the highest-scoring inning in All-Star history?

Answers

382. 1959. The experiment ended in 1962. 1960 was the only year in which one league (NL) won both games.

383. 1962, at D.C. Stadium, Washington. Other new stadiums that hosted the All-Star Game were St. Louis' Busch Memorial (1966) and Cincinnati's Riverfront (1970).

384. Casey Stengel, 6.

385. The DiMaggio's. Vince, Joe, and Dom.

386. Lance Parrish, Detroit (AL), 7/13/82. Parrish threw out Steve Sax, Ozzie Smith, and Al Oliver.

387. Fred Lynn, California (AL), connected off Atlee Hammaker of San Francisco (NL) in the 3rd inning of the 1983 contest, the 50th anniversary game at Chicago's Comiskey Park. The AL broke an 11-year losing streak with a 13-3 rout.

388. Manny Trillo, 2nd baseman, with Philadelphia (NL) in 1982 and Cleveland (AL) in 1983.

389. San Francisco's Atlee Hammaker gave up all 7 of the AL's third-inning runs in the 1983 game, retiring just one batter.

Questions

390. *What World Series saw the most records broken?*

391. *Who replaced Tony Kubek at shortstop after he was struck in the throat by Bill Virdon's bad-hop grounder during the 7th game of the 1960 World Series?*

392. *Who was the first black to pitch and win a World Series game?*

393. *What two teams played in the first World Series?*

394. *Who was the Yankee left fielder who watched Bill Mazeroski's home run disappear into Schenley Park to end the 1960 World Series?*

395. *What pitcher has the most World Series victories without a defeat?*

396. *Who made the only unassisted triple play in World Series history?*

397. *Who hit the first grand slam in World Series play?*

398. *Who was the only player to belt five home runs in a World Series?*

Answers

THE FALL CLASSIC

390. The 1932 classic between the New York Yankees and the Chicago Cubs saw 15 records broken and two tied. Babe Ruth figured in 13 of these.

391. Joe DeMaestri.

392. Joe Black, Brooklyn, 10/1/52.

393. The Pittsburgh Pirates and the Boston Pilgrims, 1903. Boston won 5 games to 3.

394. Lawrence "Yogi" Berra. Ralph Terry threw the gopher ball as Dick Stuart, batting for Harvey Haddix, watched from the on-deck circle.

395. Vernon "Lefty" Gomez was 6-0 in the fall classic.

396. Bill Wambsganss, Cleveland 2nd baseman, 10/10/20. He caught a line drive off the bat of Brooklyn relief pitcher Clarence Mitchell. The next time up Mitchell hit into a double play. Five outs in two at bats!

397. Elmer Smith, Cleveland center fielder, 10/10/20, vs. Brooklyn.

398. Reggie Jackson, New York, vs. Los Angeles, 1977.

Questions

399. What World Series saw the largest total attendance?

400. Who was the only pitcher to throw three shutouts in the same World Series?

401. What player broke up Floyd Bevens' bid for a no-hitter in the 1947 World Series?

402. What teams were involved in the first World Series sweep?

403. What outfielder has the infamous World Series record of committing three errors in one inning?

404. What Milwaukee Braves pitcher beat the NY Yankees three times in a World Series?

405. What shortstop committed eight errors in a World Series yet was chosen the MVP of that same series?

Answers

399. The 1959 World Series, in which Los Angeles defeated Chicago in six games, was played before 420,784 fans. The single game high was 92,706 at the Coliseum on 10/6/59.

400. Christy Mathewson, NY Giants, vs. Philadelphia, 1905. In that five-game series, the entire Giant pitching staff did not allow an earned run!

401. Brooklyn's Cookie Lavagetto's two-out double in the ninth inning cost Bevens not only the no-hitter but the game as well. The Bums beat the Yanks in that fourth game of the series, 3-2.

402. The Chicago Cubs defeated the Detroit Tigers 4-0 in 1907. That series also included a 3-3, 12-inning tie in the first game.

403. Los Angeles' Willie Davis, in the 5th inning of the second game of the 1966 series against Baltimore.

404. Lew Burdette, 1957. He had three complete games and the last two were shutouts.

405. Roger Peckinpaugh, in a losing effort for Washington against Pittsburgh in the 1925 series.

Questions

406. What two pitchers lost the most games in one World Series?

407. What AL club has the distinction of being the only team ever to lose three straight World Series?

408. What team had an entire switch-hitting infield in the World Series?

409. What pitcher struck out the most batters in a World Series game?

410. Who holds the World Series record for hitting safely in the most consecutive games?

411. Who was the first National League designated hitter in World Series play?

412. Who was the oldest man ever to play in the World Series?

413. What Yankee holds the record for pitching in the most World Series games?

414. What two players share the career mark for stolen bases in the World Series?

Answers

406. George Frazier, New York, lost three games to Los Angeles in 1981. Claude "Lefty" Williams lost three for the Chicago White Sox in the eight-game 1919 series. However, Williams was a part of the infamous Black Sox Scandal that year, and one will never know if he was actually beaten by or intentionally lost to the Cincinnati Reds.

407. Detroit, 1907 through 1909. The Tigers were managed by Hughie Jennings.

408. Los Angeles, 1965-66. 1st baseman Wes Parker, 2nd baseman Jim Lefebvre, shortstop Maury Wills, and 3rd baseman Junior Gilliam.

409. Bob Gibson fanned 17 on 10/2/68 as St. Louis defeated Detroit in the first game of the series, 4-0.

410. Hank Bauer, 17.

411. Dan Driessen, Cincinnati, vs. New York, 1976. Lou Piniella DH'ed for New York.

412. Jack Quinn pitched for Philadelphia against the St. Louis Cardinals in 1930 at the age of 46.

413. Whitey Ford, 22.

414. Eddie Collins and Lou Brock, 14.

Questions

415. What pitcher completed the most games in World Series play?

416. What pitcher won the most opening games in the World Series?

417. How did the World Series come about?

418. The formation of the players' union has caused strikes and rumors of strikes, but what World Series saw the players actually go on strike?

419. In the 1927 World Series, a Hall of Fame Pirate refused to play because he was superstitious about hitting in the second spot in the lineup. Who was he?

Answers

415. Christy Mathewson, 10, in four World Series.

416. The Yankees' Red Ruffing, 5, 1932, 1936, 1938, 1939, and 1941.

417. A best-of-9 championship match between the pennant winners of the established National League and the fledgling American League arose from the demands of public opinion over who was the superior team in 1903, the Pittsburgh Pirates or the Boston Pilgrims. Boston won 5 games to 3. The best-of-7 format has been used since 1905 except for the years 1919-21, which were best-of-9 series.

418. The 1918 series between the Red Sox and the Cubs. The players held a sit-down strike prior to the fifth game to protest second-, third-, and fourth-place clubs sharing in the series receipts. Each member of the winning Red Sox received $890 and each of the Cubs $535 under the new plan, after deduction for war charities, the smallest in series history, although the original divisions were $1,102.51 and $671.09.

419. Hazen "Kiki" Cuyler.

Questions

420. *What costly step decided the World Series of 1924?*

421. *What pitcher holds the World Series mark for consecutive scoreless innings?*

422. *What batter struck out the most often in World Series play?*

423. *What rookie hit the most homers in his first World Series?*

424. *Who holds the RBI record for a single World Series game?*

425. *What two players stroked six straight hits in the World Series?*

426. *Who hit the first World Series home run?*

427. *Who is the only pitcher to appear in all seven games of a World Series?*

428. *In the 1947 Fall Classic between the Yankees and the Dodgers, two standout players of that series were gone when the 1948 season began. Who were they?*

429. *Who is the only player to stroke 10 hits in a four-game World Series?*

Answers

420. New York Giant catcher Hank Gowdy tripped on his own mask while going after Muddy Ruel's foul pop fly in the 12th inning of the seventh game on 10/10/24. Ruel subsequently doubled and scored when Washington teammate Earl McNelly's grounder took a bad hop over 3rd baseman Fred Lindstrom's head to win it all!

421. Whitey Ford, $33\frac{2}{3}$.

422. Mickey Mantle, 54 times in 65 games.

423. The Yankees' Charlie "King Kong" Keller hit 3 homers against Cincinnati in the 1939 classic.

424. New York's Bobby Richardson had 6 RBIs on 10/8/60 against Pittsburgh.

425. Goose Goslin did it for Washington against New York in 1924 while the Yanks' Thurman Munson turned the trick against the Reds in 1976.

426. Jim Sebring, Pittsburgh, vs. Boston, 10/1/03.

427. Darold Knowles, Oakland, vs. New York, 1973.

428. Neither Bill Bevens of New York nor Al Gionfriddo of Brooklyn ever played in a major league game again.

429. Babe Ruth, New York Yanks, vs. St. Louis, 1928.

Questions

430. Who was the only pitcher to hit a World Series grand slam?

431. Who has the highest lifetime World Series batting average (minimum 20 games)?

432. Who was the only player to hit four homers in two different series?

433. In 1905, all five World Series games were shutouts. Who pitched them?

434. What pitcher served up the Vic Wertz clout run down by Willie Mays in the 1954 World Series?

435. Who holds the record for the most extra-base hits in a single World Series?

436. Since its inception, what was the only year without a World Series?

437. What player hit a homer in his first and only time at bat in the World Series?

Answers

430. Baltimore hurler Dave McNally connected off Cincinnati's Wayne Granger on 10/13/70.

431. Lou Brock, .391. Pepper Martin has the mark for right-handers at .344. Both were series standouts for the St. Louis Cardinals.

432. Duke Snider, 1952 and 1955.

433. New York's Christy Mathewson pitched three and teammate Joe McGinnity, one. Philadelphia A's hurler Chief Bender notched the second-game shutout.

434. New York's Don Liddle.

435. Willie Stargell had seven for Pittsburgh against Baltimore in 1979.

436. 1904. New York Giants owner John Brush refused to jeopardize the established National League's integrity by playing a "bush league" team. Manager John McGraw supported Brush's decision because of his personal antipathy for AL president Ban Johnson.

437. Jim Mason, New York Yankee shortstop, homered off Reds' pitcher Pat Zachry on 10/19/76. Mason had not homered during the regular season that year.

Questions

438. Who is the only player to hit a home run in his first two at bats in the World Series?

439. Who was the only player to appear in a World Series game even though he did not play a single game during that regular season?

440. In the 1926 World Series the most thrilling moment came in the 7th inning of the seventh game when Grover Cleveland Alexander came on in relief to strike out Tony Lazzeri of the Yankees with the bases loaded. What pitcher did "Old Pete" relieve and who were the three runners left stranded?

441. What Hall of Famer hit into the most double plays in a World Series game?

442. What Yankee hit into the most double plays in one World Series?

443. What two pitchers with identical last names hit opposing batters on successive pitches in the World Series?

Answers

438. Gene Tenace, Oakland, vs. Cincinnati, 10/14/72. Tenace hit two more home runs in that series and set the record for slugging percentage in a seven-game series with a .913 mark.

439. Clyde McCullough, Chicago Cubs, 1945. He had been in the service during the season and was discharged in time for the fall classic. This was obviously before the current rule that prohibits such action.

440. Alexander relieved St. Louis starter Jess Haines. The Yankee runners were Earle Combs on 3rd, Bob Meusel on 2nd, and Lou Gehrig on 1st.

441. Willie Mays of New York hit into three double plays against the Yankees on 10/8/51.

442. Irv Noren of the Yankees hit into 5 double plays in the 1955 series against Brooklyn.

443. Tippy and Dennis Martinez (not related), Baltimore relievers, hit Pittsburgh's Dave Parker and Bill Robinson respectively on 10/17/79.

Questions

444. *What six teams came back from 3-1 deficits to win the World Series?*

445. *What was the longest game played in the World Series (by the clock)?*

446. *What was the longest nine-inning game played in the World Series?*

447. *Who was the oldest player to win the World Series MVP award?*

448. *What player went to bat most often in a single World Series without striking out?*

Answers

444. 1903 Boston (AL) vs. Pittsburgh (NL)
   1925 Pittsburgh (NL) vs. Washington (AL)
   1958 New York (AL) vs. Milwaukee (NL)
   1968 Detroit (AL) vs. St. Louis (NL)
   1979 Pittsburgh (NL) vs. Baltimore (AL)
   1985 Kansas City (AL) vs. St. Louis (NL).

445. The second game of the 1973 series between Oakland and the New York Mets went 12 innings and lasted 4 hours and 13 minutes, 10/14/73.

446. The fourth game of the 1979 series between Pittsburgh and Baltimore lasted 3 hours and 48 minutes, 10/13/79.

447. Willie Stargell won the MVP for Pittsburgh in 1979 at the age of 38.

448. Pittsburgh's Tim Foli went to bat 30 times against Baltimore in 1979 without fanning. In that same year, Foli played from August 18 to the last week of September without striking out.

Questions

449. What two teams used the most pitchers in one World Series inning?

450. What pitcher started the most consecutive opening games in World Series play?

451. What World Series was the first to be televised?

452. What Dodger outfielder made headlines in the 1955 series with his spectacular catch of Yogi Berra's fly ball?

453. Who holds the lifetime World Series record for batting average by a switch-hitter (minimum 50 at bats)?

454. Who is the only man to steal home twice in World Series play?

455. Who was the youngest player to appear in the World Series?

456. What was the World Series originally called?

Answers

449. Baltimore manager Earl Weaver used five pitchers in the 9th inning of the seventh game of the 1979 series against Pittsburgh. In order, the Birds used Tim Stoddard, Mike Flanagan, Don Stanhouse, Tippy Martinez, and Dennis Martinez, 10/17/79. St. Louis skipper Whitey Herzog used Bill Campbell, Jeff Lahti, Ricky Horton, Joaquin Andujar, and Bob Forsch in the 5th inning of the seventh game of the 1985 series against Kansas City. The Royals scored six times that inning in coasting to an 11-0 triumph and the world championship.

450. Whitey Ford, 4. He did it twice, 1955-58 and 1961-64.

451. The 1947 Brooklyn-New York series was televised on NBC.

452. Sandy Amoros helped clinch the seventh-game win over the Yanks on 10/4/55. Fifteen years later, Amoros was found a pauper in Manhattan.

453. Buck Weaver, .327.

454. Bob Meusel, NY Yankees, 10/6/21 and 10/7/28.

455. Fred Lindstrom, NY Giants, 1924. He was 18 years, 10 months, and 13 days as of 10/4/24.

456. The Temple Cup.

Questions

457. What pitcher has the World Series record for consecutive innings without allowing an earned run?

458. What was the first World Series played exclusively on artificial turf?

459. What batter struck out the most times in one World Series?

460. Who was the first pitcher to hit a home run in a World Series game?

461. What two players, in different series, were awarded first base by proving to the umpires that they were hit by pitches?

462. Who was the only player to steal seven bases in a World Series?

463. What player received the most World Series checks?

464. What two teams were involved in the first intracity World Series?

465. When was the last intracity World Series?

Answers

457. Waite Hoyt of the Yankees pitched 34²/₃ innings over the 1921 and 1922 series before finally allowing an earned run.

458. The 1980 series between Philadelphia and Kansas City.

459. Willie Wilson struck out 12 times for Kansas City against Philadelphia in 1980.

460. Jim Bagby, Sr., Cleveland, vs. Brooklyn, 10/10/20.

461. Vernal "Nippy" Jones, Milwaukee, 10/6/57, and Cleon Jones, NY Mets, 10/16/69. Each convinced the home plate umpire that he was hit in the foot by showing the shoe polish marks on the baseball!

462. Lou Brock, St. Louis, did it *twice,* in 1967 and 1968.

463. Frankie Crosetti, New York Yankees, 23.

464. The Chicago Cubs and the Chicago White Sox, 1906. The Pale Hose won 4-2.

465. 1956. The Yankees defeated the Dodgers, 4-3.

Questions

466. What player has collected the most World Series hits?

467. Who were the only teammates to belt grand slams in the same series?

468. What NL team has won the most Fall Classics?

469. What player had the highest batting average in one World Series?

470. What team holds the longest winning streak in World Series play?

471. Who was the youngest man to manage a World Series team?

472. What team owns the record for home runs in a single series?

473. What pitcher fanned the most batters in a series relief appearance?

474. Who holds the record for RBIs in one series?

475. What two players share the record for the most hits in a World Series?

Answers

466. Yogi Berra, 71 hits in 14 series.

467. New York's Yogi Berra and Bill Skowron, vs. Brooklyn, 1956.

468. The St. Louis Cardinals, 9.

469. Babe Ruth hit at a .625 clip in the Yanks' four-game sweep of the Cards in 1928.

470. The Yankees, 12. The Bronx Bombers swept the Pirates (1927), Cards (1928) and Cubs (1932) to set this mark.

471. Joe Cronin, age 27, with Washington in their 1933 series loss to the Giants.

472. The 1956 Yankees hit twelve homers against Brooklyn.

473. Baltimore's Moe Drabowsky fanned 11 Dodgers in 6⅔ innings, 10/5/66.

474. Bobby Richardson, 12, with New York against Pittsburgh in 1960.

475. Bobby Richardson, 1960, and Lou Brock, 1967, each had 13 hits.

Questions

476. Who holds the World Series record for most hits in a 9-inning game?

477. Who holds the World Series record for most singles in one game?

478. Who is the only player to have two 4-hit games in the same series?

479. When was the longest string of years that the World Series went seven games?

480. What year saw the only "all-St. Louis" World Series?

481. What two players hit home runs to win back-to-back 1-0 World Series games?

482. Who was the first pitcher to win three games in a seven-game series?

Answers

476. Paul Molitor, Milwaukee, had 5 hits against St. Louis on 10/12/82.

477. Paul Molitor, Milwaukee, had 5 singles against St. Louis on 10/12/82.

478. Robin Yount, Milwaukee, vs. St. Louis, 1982.

479. Four years, 1955-58.

480. 1944. The Cardinals defeated the Browns, 4-2.

481. Baltimore's Paul Blair and Frank Robinson homered to give the 1966 Orioles consecutive 1-0 wins in the last two games of their sweep over Los Angeles. Over the years, two other men have won 1-0 games with a homer. In 1923, Casey Stengel homered to help the Giants beat the Yanks in the third game of their six-game series loss. In 1949, Tommy Henrich did the same as the Yanks beat Brooklyn in the first game of their 4-1 series victory.

482. Babe Adams, Pittsburgh, vs. Detroit, 1909.

Questions

483. Who was the only player to be picked off twice in a World Series game?

484. What four men played on three different world champion franchises?

Answers

483. Max Flack, Chicago Cubs, vs. Boston, 1918. He was picked off by Babe Ruth in the fourth game, 9/9/18.

484. Leslie "Bullet Joe" Bush   1913 Philadelphia (AL)
                                       1918 Boston (AL)
                                       1923 New York (AL)

      Wally Schang   1913, 1930 Philadelphia (AL)
                                       1918 Boston (AL)
                                       1921, 1923 New York (AL)

      Stuffy McInnis   1910-11, 1913 Philadelphia (AL)
                                         1918 Boston (AL)
                                       1925 Pittsburgh (NL)

      Lonnie Smith   1980 Philadelphia (NL)
                                       1982 St. Louis (NL)
                                       1985 Kansas City (NL).

Sidelights

FOR THE ANNUAL SHOWCASE

Sneaky Fast

At 6'2" and 215 pounds, and with most of the weight distributed above his piano legs, many picture Babe Ruth as having been slow afoot. To the contrary, Babe was deceptively fast. In his 22-year career, the Bambino stole 123 bases. And of his 714 lifetime home runs, 10 were inside-the-park specials!

Parallels in Pinstripes

Babe Ruth and Reggie Jackson are the only men to have hit 3 home runs in a single World Series game. Ruth did it twice. These feats had the following parallels:

1. Both men were playing for the Yankees.
2. Both men were right fielders.
3. Both men were left-handed.
4. Jackson hit his three on the first pitch; Ruth hit 2 of his 3 on the first pitch.
5. Both men were age 31 at the time. (Ruth also did it at age 33).

4.

BEYOND THE FOUL LINES

Questions

THE ACE OF CLUBS

485. *What was the original name of the Houston Astros?*

486. *How did the Cleveland Indians get their nickname?*

487. *Who was named the Yankees' first team captain since Lou Gehrig?*

488. *Where did the Phillies play their home games before Veterans Stadium?*

489. *What was the only year the St. Louis Browns won the AL pennant and who was their manager?*

Answers

THE ACE OF CLUBS

485. The Colt 45's. The name was changed when the club moved to the Astrodome in 1965.

486. In honor of Louis Sockalexis, a full-blooded Penobscot who played for the Cleveland Spiders. His career ended in 1898 when he saved the life of a child in a runaway baby carriage. In doing so, he crushed his foot, an injury that ended his career. For his heroism, the team was later renamed the Indians.

487. Thurman Munson.

488. Shibe Park, later renamed Connie Mack Stadium.

489. 1944, Luke Sewell.

Questions

490. *How many current major league parks can you name?*

491. *Where is the "Chinese Wall" located?*

Answers

490.

	American League
Baltimore Orioles	Memorial Stadium
Boston Red Sox	Fenway Park
California Angels	Anaheim Stadium
Chicago White Sox	Comiskey Park
Cleveland Indians	Municipal Stadium
Detroit Tigers	Tiger Stadium
Kansas City Royals	Royals Stadium
Milwaukee Brewers	County Stadium
Minnesota Twins	Hubert H. Humphrey Metrodome
New York Yankees	Yankee Stadium
Oakland A's	Oakland-Alameda County Stadium
Seattle Mariners	Kingdome
Texas Rangers	Arlington Stadium
Toronto Blue Jays	Exhibition Stadium

	National League
Atlanta Braves	Atlanta-Fulton County Stadium
Chicago Cubs	Wrigley Field
Cincinnati Reds	Riverfront Stadium
Houston Astros	Astrodome
Los Angeles Dodgers	Dodger Stadium
Montreal Expos	Olympic Stadium
New York Mets	Shea Stadium
Philadelphia Phillies	Veterans Stadium
Pittsburgh Pirates	Three Rivers Stadium
St. Louis Cardinals	Busch Stadium
San Diego Padres	San Diego-Jack Murphy Stadium
San Francisco Giants	Candlestick Park.

491. The left field fence in Boston's Fenway Park. It has also been dubbed the "Green Monster."

Questions

492. *What was the widest spread in games between a pennant winner and the second-place team?*

493. *What major league team never drew one million paid fans in a season?*

494. *What club won the most games in one season?*

495. *What was the first team to rip up the artificial turf and replace it with grass?*

496. *Where did the Reds play their baseball before moving to Riverfront Stadium?*

497. *Who were the predecessors of the Milwaukee Brewers?*

498. *What was the first team to draw two million fans at home and away?*

499. *In what stadium did the Seattle Pilots play their home games?*

500. *Who was the last active Brooklyn Dodger?*

501. *What are the four clubs that showed a paid attendance increase of one million fans in one year?*

502. *What club was the first to move to another city?*

Answers

492. The 1902 Pittsburgh Pirates finished 27½ games ahead of the Brooklyn Robins.

493. The Philadelphia Athletics.

494. The Chicago Cubs won 116 games (36 losses) in 1906. Cleveland holds the AL mark with 111 wins (43 losses) in 1954.

495. San Francisco, 1979. In a move that cost $868,000, the Giants reluctantly agreed with the football 49ers to do the deed to Candlestick Park.

496. Crosley Field, originally named Redland Field.

497. The 1969 Seattle Pilots. A bankruptcy court escorted them to Milwaukee.

498. The 1966 Los Angeles Dodgers.

499. Sicks Stadium.

500. Bob Aspromonte, who retired in 1971. He became a "Bum" at the age of 18.

501. 1946 New York Yankees
     1948 Cleveland Indians
     1965 Houston Astros
     1978 San Francisco Giants.

502. The Braves moved from Boston to Milwaukee in 1953.

Questions

503. *What team was known as the Nats?*

504. *What club had a fan so loyal that he sat on a flagpole in their behalf for 117 days?*

505. *What team had the frustrating misfortune of losing 44 one-run games in one season?*

506. *What club used the most players in one season?*

507. *Where did the Pirates play their games before Forbes Field?*

508. *Why do the Cincinnati Reds always draw the opening game of the season?*

509. *Where is baseball's largest scoreboard located?*

510. *How many times has Milwaukee been in the major leagues?*

Answers

503. Washington. Before they were dubbed the Senators, they were called the Nationals. Sportswriters shortened it to the Nats.

504. The 1949 Cleveland Indians. From 5/31/49, when the club was in fourth place, to 9/25/49, when they were mathematically eliminated from the pennant race, Charley Lupica spent 117 days atop a flagpole in a fruitless effort waiting for Cleveland to regain first place.

505. The 1968 Chicago White Sox. They also won 30 games by the same margin.

506. The 1915 Philadelphia A's tried 56 men, and it still didn't work. They finished dead last, 58½ games behind Boston.

507. Exposition Park. The Bucs moved to Forbes Field in 1909.

508. The honor goes to the Reds as baseball's oldest major league franchise.

509. Detroit's Tiger Stadium.

510. Five times. 1878 in the NL, 1884 in the Union Association, 1891 jointure with Cincinnati in the American Association, 1953 in the NL again, and 1970 in the AL.

Questions

511. What year saw the first attempt to move major league baseball to the Pacific Coast?

512. Who were the members of the first all-black major league outfield?

513. What team holds the record for one-run victories in the same season?

514. What was the only team that swept the league championship series and the World Series?

515. What was the first club to wear double knit uniforms?

516. What were the three clubs that hit four consecutive homers in an inning?

517. What team holds the record for home runs in one season by two teammates?

518. What is the major leagues' longest continuing franchise?

Answers

511. The St. Louis Browns' attempt to settle in Los Angeles was terminated when the Japanese bombed Pearl Harbor in 1941.

512. Left fielder Monte Irvin, center fielder Willie Mays, and right fielder Hank Thompson of the 1951 Giants. Thompson replaced the injured Don Mueller in the World Series against the Yankees.

513. The 1978 San Francisco Giants, 42.

514. The 1976 Cincinnati Reds.

515. The Pittsburgh Pirates became the first club to do so when it moved to Three Rivers Stadium in July, 1970.

516. Milwaukee Braves, 7th inning, 6/8/61, Mathews, Aaron, Adcock, Thomas
Cleveland Indians, 6th inning, 7/31/63, Held, Ramos, Francona, Brown
Minnesota Twins, 11th inning, 5/2/64, Oliva, Allison, Hall, Killebrew.

517. The 1961 New York Yankees featured Roger Maris (61) and Mickey Mantle (54) who combined for 115 home runs.

518. The Chicago Cubs have been in the "Windy City" since the NL's inception in 1876.

Questions

519. What were the New York Yankees originally called?

520. What stadium had a sign under the scoreboard that read "Hit Sign—Win Suit"?

521. What was the original name of Tiger Stadium?

522. What was the earliest date a team clinched the pennant?

523. Who played 3rd base in the famous Chicago Cub combination "Tinker to Evers to Chance"?

524. Which club had seven .300 hitters in one year?

Answers

519. **The New York Highlanders.** In 1903, the Franchise was moved from Baltimore to "The Big Apple" where they played their games at Hilltop Park. The Highlanders became the Yankees in 1907.

520. **Ebbets Field, Brooklyn.** The sponsor was Al Stark.

521. **Bennett Park.** It was later changed to Navin Field and later still to Briggs Stadium.

522. **The 1941 New York Yankees** under the leadership of Joe McCarthy clinched the AL pennant on September 4th. They finished 17 games ahead of runner-up Boston.

523. **Harry Steinfeldt.**

524. **The 1927 Philadelphia Athletics.**

CF	Al Simmons	.392	3B	Sammy Hale	.313
LF	Ty Cobb	.357	SS	Joe Boley	.311
C	Mickey Cochrane	.338	RF	Walt French	.304
1B	Jimmy Dykes	.324			

The team also had three other .300 hitters who failed to qualify for the batting title. They were Eddie Collins (.338), Zack Wheat (.324), and Jimmie Foxx (.323). Despite this .303 team batting average, the A's finished in second place, 19 games behind the NY Yankees.

Questions

525. *What is the record number of batters to come to the plate in one inning?*

526. *What team pounded out the highest season batting average?*

527. *What three teams won over 102 games and did not win the pennant?*

528. *What major league park has the largest seating capacity?*

529. *Who was the only man to play for the Braves in Boston, Milwaukee, and Atlanta?*

530. *What is the oldest ballpark still in use?*

531. *What team introduced tricolor uniforms to baseball?*

Answers

525. 23. It was first set on 9/6/1883 by Chicago against Detroit in the 7th inning. On 6/18/53, the Boston Red Sox tied the mark against the Tigers.

526. The 1894 Philadelphia club batted a whopping .343!

527.

1902 Chicago Cubs	104-49	6½ games behind Pittsburgh
1942 Brooklyn Dodgers	104-50	2 games behind St. Louis
1954 NY Yankees	103-51	8 games behind Cleveland.

528. Cleveland's Municipal Stadium, 76,713.

529. Eddie Mathews.

530. Comiskey Park, Chicago, first opened in 1910.

531. The Oakland A's. Gold, white, and forest green.

Questions

SOMEHOW THEY MANAGED

532. Who were the only two managers traded for each other?

533. What Yankee manager was fired after winning the AL pennant?

534. Who was the only non-Yankee manager to win a pennant between 1949 and 1964?

535. Who were the only two managers to win pennants for three different teams?

536. Besides ex-Yankee manager Billy Martin, who was the only manager to pilot the same club four different times?

537. What manager and coach erased the chalk off the coaching box on the 3rd base line?

Answers

SOMEHOW THEY MANAGED

532. In 1959, Jimmy Dykes went from Detroit to Cleveland for Joe Gordon.

533. Yogi Berra, 1964. He was replaced by Johnny Keane whose Cardinals had just defeated New York in the World Series.

534. Al Lopez. He piloted the 1954 Cleveland and 1959 Chicago teams to pennants.

535. Bill McKechnie —1925 Pittsburgh (NL), 1928 St. Louis (NL), 1939-40 Cincinnati (NL).
Dick Williams—1967 Boston (AL), 1972-73 Oakland (AL), 1984 San Diego (NL).
Only McKechnie's Pirates and Williams' A's won the World Series, however.

536. Danny Murtaugh, Pittsburgh, 1957-64, 1967, 1970-71, and 1973-76.

537. Leo Durocher.

Questions

538. *What season saw the most playing managers and who were they?*

539. *Who holds the record for managing the same team the longest?*

540. *The Texas Rangers set an AL record in 1977 by hiring four managers in the course of the season. Who were those four men?*

541. *Who was the major leagues' first playing manager?*

542. *What manager holds the record for World Series wins?*

Answers

538. 1934, 10, 6 in the NL and 4 in the AL. They were:

National

Frankie Frisch	St. Louis
Charlie Grimm	Chicago
Bob O'Farrell	Cincinnati
Bill Terry	New York
Pie Traynor	Pittsburgh
Jimmie Wilson	Philadelphia

American

Mickey Cochrane	Detroit
Joe Cronin	Washington
Jimmy Dykes	Chicago
Rogers Hornsby	St. Louis.

539. "The Tall Tactician," Connie Mack. From 1901 through 1950, Mack managed the Philadelphia A's. He was also the head man for Pittsburgh, 1894-96.

540. Frank Lucchesi (31-31), Eddie Stanky (1-0), Connie Ryan (2-4), and Billy Hunter (60-33) combined for a 94-68 second-place finish, 8 games behind Kansas City.

541. Cap Anson, 1st baseman, Chicago (NL), 1879.

542. Casey Stengel, 37.

Questions

543. What manager twice *lifted pitchers who had no-hitters going into the ninth inning?*

544. What manager *never left the dugout during a game?*

545. Who was the last major league playing manager?

546. Who succeeded Connie Mack as manager of the Philadelphia A's?

547. Who holds the record for managing different. teams in the majors?

548. Who was the only major league manager to coach in the NFL?

549. What major league manager had a son on his team?

Answers

543. Preston Gomez lifted Clay Kirby on 7/21/70 for Clarence Gaston who struck out. Then on 9/4/74 Gomez lifted Houston pitcher Don Wilson for Tommy Helms who grounded out. Not only did the Padres' and Astros' hurlers lose their bids for no-hitters, but their teams lost the games as well at the hands of 9th-inning relievers!

544. Connie Mack. He positioned his club on the field by waving a scorecard. It may also be noted that manager Mack called every player "Mister" and always wore street clothes to the game.

545. Pete Rose, 1984-85 Cincinnati Reds.

546. Jimmy Dykes, 1951.

547. Frank Bancroft, 7, although one of those teams was in the American Association. He and Jimmy Dykes each managed 6 NL and AL teams.

548. Hugo Bezdek managed the Pittsburgh Pirates from 1917 to 1919 and was the head coach for the Cleveland Rams in 1937-38.

549. Connie Mack, whose son Earl played under his father in 1910-11, and 1914.

Questions

550. Who was the only manager to manage against his son?

551. Who were the four rookie managers to win 100 games?

552. Who was the last playing manager to win a pennant and a batting title in the same year?

553. What Hall of Fame manager chalked up the most victories?

554. Who managed the Seattle Pilots in their only year of existence?

555. Who was the only manager to win the World Series in both leagues?

556. What manager was fired with his team in first place?

557. What former Cub 1st baseman returned to Chicago and managed them to their last pennant in 1945?

558. What Hall of Famer managed the Washington Senators to their last pennant?

Answers

550. Maury Wills, Seattle, managed against his son Elliot "Bump" Wills of Texas in 1980.

551.

Mickey Cochrane	1934 Detroit	101 wins
Ralph Houk	1961 NY Yanks	109 wins
Sparky Anderson	1970 Cincinnati	102 wins
Dick Howser	1980 NY Yanks	103 wins.

552. Cap Anson, Chicago, hit .399 in 1881.

553. Connie Mack registered 3,776 wins in his 53 years of managing.

554. Joe Schultz.

555. Sparky Anderson, 1975-76 Cincinnati (NL) and 1984 Detroit (AL).

556. Pat Corrales. He was replaced by Phils' General Manager Paul Owens on 7/18/83 and hired by Cleveland later that same season. The Phils ended up in the World Series where they lost to Baltimore in five games.

557. Charlie Grimm.

558. Joe Cronin, 1933.

Questions

559. Who was the last man to win a pennant as a playing manager?

560. Who was the last first-year manager to win a pennant?

561. What franchise had a different manager every year from 1959 to 1971?

562. Who was the only manager to homer on the first pitch thrown to him as a player?

563. Who managed the most seasons without winning a pennant?

564. What manager had the most seasons with a record above .500?

565. Who is the only manager to win 100 games in each league?

Answers

559. Lou Boudreau played shortstop and managed the 1948 Cleveland Indians to a world championship over Boston, 4-2.

560. Jim Frey, Kansas City, 1980. Dallas Green, Frey's counterpart in that series, was in his first full year with Philadelphia after having managed the Phillies for part of 1979.

561. The Kansas City/Oakland Athletics.

562. Chuck Tanner, Milwaukee Braves, 4/12/55.

563. Gene Mauch, 23, 1960-82.

564. John McGraw, piloted his team to an above-.500 record 29 out of 34 seasons, an outstanding .853 percentage.

565. Sparky Anderson, Cincinnati (NL), 1970, 1975-76, and Detroit (AL), 1984.

Questions

MOONLIGHTING

566. Who has the distinction of hitting a home run off Sandy Koufax and catching a touchdown pass from Y. A. Tittle?

567. What All-American collegiate basketball twins played major league baseball?

568. Who was the only major league player to win college football's Heisman Trophy?

569. Who was the only player to appear on two championship teams in different sports in two consecutive seasons?

570. What member of the NFL Hall of Fame hit a home run in his first at bat in major league baseball?

571. What slugger was drafted to play in three different professional sports?.

572. He was an All-American quarterback at the University of Mississippi and caught for the NY Yankees. Who was he?

573. What major league pitcher and former Kansas University quarterback played in the same backfield with Gale Sayers?

Answers

MOONLIGHTING

566. Al Dark hit the round tripper while with the NY Giants and caught the touchdown pass as a collegian at Louisiana State University.

567. Eddie and Johnny O'Brien both played with Pittsburgh in the 1950's.

568. Vic Janowicz won the Heisman in his junior year with Ohio State in 1950. He played his major league ball with Pittsburgh in 1953-54. He also played with the NFL Washington Redskins in 1954-55.

569. Gene Conley pitched for the NL representative in the World Series, Milwaukee, in 1957-58. Conley also played on the NBA world champion Boston Celtics during the 1958-59 season.

570. Clarence "Ace" Parker, Philadelphia A's, 4/30/37.

571. Dave Winfield was drafted by the NL San Diego Padres, the NFL Minnesota Vikings, and the NBA Atlanta Hawks and ABA Utah Stars.

572. Jake Gibbs. A damn Yankee and a Rebel to boot!

573. Steve Renko.

Questions

574. What NL pitcher pulled down over 700 rebounds for the Detroit Pistons after graduating from Notre Dame?

575. What Cy Young Award winner once toured with the Harlem Globetrotters?

576. Who was the first man to play for the NFL New York Giants and major league baseball's New York Giants?

577. Who was the only player to hit two home runs in the World Series and also play in the Rose Bowl?

578. What NFL coach, owner, and player played 12 games with the NY Yankees?

579. What major league players also performed in the NBA?

580. Who was the only major leaguer to play in the NFL Super Bowl?

Answers

574. Ron Reed.

575. Ferguson Jenkins, 6'5" and 205 lbs.

576. Jim Thorpe.

577. Chuck Essegian, Los Angeles, 1959. Both clouts were pinch-hits. Essegian was the Stanford quarterback from 1950 to 1952. His 1952 Rose Bowl appearance was a disastrous 40-7 loss to Illinois. His baseball career saw him play with six different clubs in the six years he played.

578. George "Papa Bear" Halas, Chicago Bears.

579.
Howie Schultz	1949-53
Gene Conley	1952-64
Dick Ricketts	1955-58
Cotton Nash	1964-65 (also played in the ABA)
Dave DeBusschere	1964-74
Ron Reed	1965-67

Chuck Connors played in the National Basketball League (NBL) in 1945-46 and the Basketball Association of America (BAA) in 1946-48. Several other players participated in the NBL and/or BAA.

580. Tom Brown was an outfielder-1st baseman on the 1963 Washington Senators. He was a free safety for Green Bay in the first two Super Bowls (1967-68).

Questions

581. *What Yankee pitcher was an All-American football player at Georgia?*

582. *What NFL Hall of Famer gave up two of Babe Ruth's 60 homers in 1927?*

583. *What four NFL Hall of Famers also played major league baseball?*

584. *Who was the only NFL championship coach to play in a World Series?*

585. *Who was the only Olympic gold medalist to play in the World Series?*

586. *What was the last city to win the World Series and the Stanley Cup the same year?*

587. *What was the last city to win the World Series and the Super Bowl the same year?*

588. *What was the last city to win the World Series and the NBA championship within a year?*

Answers

581. Spurgeon "Spud" Chandler. As a Yankee pitcher, he holds that club's greatest won-lost percentage for a pitcher with over 100 decisions (109-43, .717). On the gridiron, Chandler once booted a 92-yard punt and was voted Georgia's greatest athlete ever.

582. Ernie Nevers, St. Louis Browns.

583. Jim Thorpe, Ernie Nevers, Ace Parker, and George Halas.

584. Earle "Greasy" Neale. He played for Cincinnati in the 1919 series and was the head coach of the NFL champion Philadelphia Eagles in 1948 and 1949.

585. Jim Thorpe was a gold medal winner at Stockholm in 1912 and played for the NY Giants in the 1917 series against Chicago.

586. New York City, 1933. The Giants and the NHL Rangers.

587. Pittsburgh, 1979. the Pirates and the NFL Steelers.

588. Los Angeles. The 1981 Dodgers and the 1981-82 NBA Lakers.

Questions

"...AND HERE'S THE PITCH"

589. Who was the famous voice of the old Brooklyn Dodgers?

590. What stadium announcer made the famous plea over the loudspeaker, "Will the ladies and gentlemen in the center field bleachers please remove their clothing"?

591. Who were the NY Giant television and radio broadcasters during the 1951 play-off series when Bobby Thomson struck his "shot heard 'round the world"?

592. Who broadcast the first major league game on radio?

593. What famous announcer initiated the home run call "It's going, going, gone!"?

594. What announcer won a $20.00 bet by diving 90 feet into the Chase Hotel swimming pool in St. Louis?

595. Who was the first Canadian to play for the Montreal Expos?

596. What sportscaster first asked, "Did you ever notice how often a man who makes an outstanding play for the third out turns out to be the first man up in the next half-inning?"

Answers

589. Red Barber. He began broadcasting games for "dem Bums" in 1939.

590. Tex Rickard, announcer for the Brooklyn Dodgers.

591. Ernie Harwell did the TV telecast while Russ Hodges called the shot for radio.

592. Harold Arlin, 8/5/21 over KDKA in Pittsburgh. The Pirates beat the Phillies, 8-5. Arlin was the grandfather of major league pitcher Steve Arlin (1969-74).

593. Mel Allen, long-time Yankee announcer.

594. Bob Prince, Pittsburgh broadcaster, 1969.

595. Claude Raymond, 1969. He later broadcast the Expo games in French for a Montreal station.

596. Mel Allen.

Questions

PROS IN PROSE

597. *What rhyme was associated with the 1948 Boston Braves?*

598. *The first man pictured on the cover of* Sports Illustrated *was a future Hall of Famer. Who was he?*

599. *Who wrote the poem "Baseball's Sad Lexicon" and what double play combination did it honor?*

600. *Who wrote the baseball poetic legend "Casey at the Bat"?*

Answers

PROS IN PROSE

597. There were two versions. "Spahn and Sain and pray for rain" was one. Also, "Spahn and Sain and two days of rain."

598. Milwaukee slugger Eddie Mathews was featured on the cover of that first copy of *Sports Illustrated*, dated August 16, 1954. Also pictured on that cover were New York Giant catcher Wes Westrum and umpire Augie Donatelli. The three were at home plate at a game at Milwaukee's County Stadium.

599. Franklin Pierce Adams. The poem went as follows:

These are the saddest of possible words,
Tinker-to-Evers-to-Chance.
Trio of Bear Cubs fleeter than birds,
Tinker-to-Evers-to-Chance.

Ruthlessly pricking our gonfalon bubble,
Making a Giant hit into a double,
Words that are weighty with nothing but trouble,
Tinker-to-Evers-to-Chance.

600. Ernest Lawrence Thayer. It first appeared in the *San Francisco Examiner* on June 3, 1888. The sequel, "Riley on the Mound," was written and narrated by actor/comedian Foster Brooks.

Questions

601. Who portrayed the Bambino in the movie The Babe Ruth Story?

602. Who is given credit for the adage, "Hit 'em where they ain't"?

603. What player was responsible for the phrase, "Home run hitters drive Cadillacs; singles hitters drive Fords"?

604. Where can a baseball fan find the following poem?

> "Now listen young fans and you shall hear
> Of a fireball pitcher named Vander Meer.
> He threw no-hitters, two in a row
> And then he ran into all sorts of woe."

605. In the famous action picture of Ty Cobb stealing third, who is the 3rd baseman attempting to tag the Georgia Peach?

606. Who introduced E. L. Thayer's "Casey at the Bat"?

Answers

601. William Bendix. Years earlier, Bendix had been dismissed as a Yankee bat boy. Bendix was fired for obtaining, at the Babe's request, a great number of hot dogs which Ruth ate prior to a game.

602. William Henry "Wee Willie" Keeler.

603. Home run hitter Ralph Kiner.

604. In Jack Newcombe's book on baseball's fastest pitchers, entitled *The Fireballers*.

605. Jimmy Austin, New York Highlanders.

606. Rudy Vallee.

Questions

607. *Where can one find the following verse?*

    "The ball once struck off
    Away flied the boy
    To the next desir'd post
    And then home with joy!"

608. *Who asked the question, "Is Brooklyn still in the league?"*

609. *What 11-year veteran turned successfully to movie and TV bad guy roles? He appeared in several episodes of the* Superman *series and many roles in* The Untouchables.

610. *What former Dodger 1st baseman became a successful television star?*

611. *Who were the Hollywood actresses the following players married?*

    Joe DiMaggio
    Leo Durocher
    Rube Marquard
    Don Hoak
    Lefty Gomez

612. *What former player and manager made the famous statement, "Nice guys finish last"?*

Answers

607. From *Little Pretty Pocket Book,* a British publication found under the one word "baseball," almost 100 years before Cooperstown's Abner Doubleday!

608. Bill Terry, NY Giants player-manager in 1934.

609. Johnny Beradino.

610. Chuck Connors, who starred in the shows *Branded* and *The Rifleman,* among others.

611. Joe DiMaggio   Marilyn Monroe
     Leo Durocher   Laraine Day
     Rube Marquard   Blossom Seeley
     Don Hoak   Jill Corey
     Lefty Gomez   June O'Dea.

612. Leo Durocher.

Questions

613. *Who wrote the following books on baseball?*

Fear Strikes Out
The Education of a Baseball Player
Me and the Spitter
I Never Had It Made *and*
   Wait 'Till Next Year
No Big Deal
Baseball is a Funny Game
It's Good To Be Alive
Screwball
My War with Baseball
The Long Season *and* The Pennant Race
Ball Four, Ball Five, *and*
   I'm Glad You Didn't Take It Personally
Three and Two
Pitching in a Pinch
Joe, Ya Could Have Made Us Proud
The Bronx Zoo
My Turn at Bat
The American Diamond
Voices from the Great Black
   Baseball Leagues
Eight Men Out
Even the Browns

Answers

613. Jimmy Piersall   Jim Bouton
     Mickey Mantle   Tom Gorman
     Gaylord Perry   Christy Mathewson
     Jackie Robinson Joe Pepitone
     Mark Fidrych   Sparky Lyle & Peter Golenbock
     Joe Garagiola   Ted Williams
     Roy Campanella Branch Rickey
     Tug McGraw   John Holway
     Rogers Hornsby Eliot Asinof
     Jim Brosnan   William B. Mead.

Questions

TRADE WINDS

614. *Who were the teams involved in the biggest trade and how many players were swapped?*

615. *What Los Angeles Dodger vice-president and loving father once traded away his own son?*

616. *What controversial pitcher played for seven different managers in 1977?*

617. *What four players share the record for playing with the most clubs?*

618. *What pitcher of the 1940s and 1950s hurled for all three New York clubs?*

Answers

TRADE WINDS

614. The NY Yankees and the Baltimore Orioles traded a total of 17 players on 11/18/54.

615. Al Campanis traded son Jim to Kansas City in 1969.

616. Dock Ellis played for Billy Martin in New York, Jack McKeon and Bobby Winkles in Oakland, and Frank Lucchesi, Eddie Stanky, Connie Ryan, and Billy Hunter in Texas.

617. Outfielder Tommy Davis and pitchers Ken Brett, Bob Miller, and Dick Littlefield all played for ten teams during their big league careers. Littlefield, however, accomplished this when there were only 16 teams in the majors.

618. Sal Maglie.

Questions

619. *Who were the first two players to play for two different teams on the same day?*

620. *Who is the only player to play for two different teams in two different cities on the same day?*

621. *What manager and catcher, who were traded for each other, ended up together on a world champion team two years after the trade?*

Answers

619. The Cubs' Max Flack and the Cardinals' Cliff Heathcote were traded for each other between games of a morning-afternoon doubleheader on 5/30/22. Both men played the afternoon game in their new uniforms.

620. Joel Youngblood, traded from New York to Montreal on 8/4/82. Traded in the middle of the game, Youngblood gave the Mets a fond farewell by driving in the game-winning run against the Cubs. He then flew to Philadelphia where he got a base hit for the Expos.

621. Oakland shipped manager Chuck Tanner to Pittsburgh for catcher Manny Sanguillen before the 1977 season. Sanguillen was shipped back to the Bucs in 1978 and was a member of the 1979 World Series champions piloted by Tanner.

Questions

THE MEN IN BLUE

622. *Who umpired the most World Series (18) and World Series games (104)?*

623. *What two umpires spent the most seasons on the diamond in their respective leagues?*

624. *Who was the major league's first black man in blue?*

625. *What umpire was called "The Old Arbitrator"?*

626. *What umpire gave the job of calling balls and strikes to a player?*

627. *What umpire left the blue garb to become the National League president?*

628. *What umpire once managed the Cincinnati Reds and the Chicago Cubs?*

629. *What umpire played pro football with the Detroit Lions?*

630. *Who are the only father and son to umpire in the big leagues?*

631. *He was a Pirate catcher in the 1940s. He was the umpire behind the plate the night the Pirates' Harvey Haddix threw 12 perfect innings in Milwaukee. He was a base umpire the day Stan Musial got his 3,000th hit. Who was he?*

Answers

THE MEN IN BLUE

622. National League umpire Bill Klem.

623. In the NL, Bill Klem umped from 1905 to 1941. AL ump Tom Connolly worked from 1901 to 1931.

624. Emmett Ashford, AL. The first black NL ump was Art Williams.

625. NL Hall of Fame umpire Bill Klem.

626. Red Ormsby, 1946. Ormsby was gassed in World War I and suffered occasionally from blurred vision and dizzy spells. One afternoon he asked Birdie Tebbetts, the Detroit catcher, to call the pitches until he recovered. Tebbetts called for three outs and then passed the word to Chicago receiver Mike Tresh, who called for two more outs. Ormsby then recovered, informed Tresh, and the game, never interrupted, continued.

627. John Heydler.

628. Hank O'Day.

629. Ron Luciano.

630. Jerry Crawford, now active, is the son of the retired Shag Crawford.

631. Vinnie Smith.

Sidelights

FOR BEYOND THE FOUL LINES

First Guessers at Last!

The St. Louis Browns once permitted their fans to manage a regular season game by using signs!

Casey Could Play the Game

Casey at the bat did not always strike out. With the NY Giants in the 1923 World Series, Casey Stengel came to bat in the top of the 9th inning of the first game with the score tied 4-4 against the Yankees. He hit an inside-the-park home run to win it for the Giants. As he rounded 3rd base his shoe almost came off. As he approached home plate, he was reeling from side to side. With a head-first slide, Stengel beat the throw by an eyelash! Stengel's third game home run gave the Giants a 1-0 win and a 2-1 edge in the series, but the Yankees came back to win it in six games.

Breakfast and Baseball

Some big league clubs served breakfast to swing shift customers during World War II in order that they might enjoy coffee with their morning baseball.

Never on Sunday

The first Sunday game at which the fans had to pay to see major league action was played on July 1, 1917. They saw Brooklyn beat Philadelphia 3-2.

A Governor's Order

In congratulating the 1978 World Champion Yankees, New York Governor Hugh Carey closed his telegram with the phrase, "Splice the main brace." This is an old Royal Navy order that means, "Give the hands an extra rum ration."

Too Hot to Handle

Since entering the National League in 1962, the New York Mets' problems at finding a regular 3rd baseman are notorious. In their first 19 seasons of existence, the Mets tried no fewer than 67 men at the hot corner before finally having success with Hubie Brooks, who played the bulk of the games between 1981 and 1984. After the 1984 season, the Mets promptly traded Brooks to Montreal. Here is the list of the 78 men who have played 3rd base for the Mets over the years:

Bill Almon	Ed Bressoud
Sandy Alomar	Hubie Brooks
*Tucker Ashford	Jerry Buchek
Bob Aspromonte	Larry Burright
*Wally Backman	Elio Chacon
*Bob Bailor	*Kelvin Chapman
Ken Boswell	Ed Charles
Ken Boyer	Kevin Collins

Cliff Cook
Mike Cubbage
Sammy Drake
Chico Fernandez
Sergio Ferrer
Doug Flynn
Tim Foli
Leo Foster
Joe Foy
Jim Fregosi
*Ron Gardenhire
Wayne Garrett
Wayne Graham
Pumpsie Green
Jerry Grote
Richie Hebner
Jack Heidemann
Bob Heise
Rick Herscher
Jim Hickman
Chuck Hiller
Ron Hunt
*Clint Hurdle
Bob Johnson
*Howard Johnson
*Ross Jones
Rod Kanehl
Dave Kingman
Bobby Klaus
*Ray Knight
Gary Kolb

Phil Linz
Elliot Maddox
Phil Mankowski
Felix Mantilla
Teddy Martinez
*Kevin Mitchell
Joe Mock
Al Moran
Jose Moreno
Danny Napoleon
Charlie Neal
Amos Otis
Bobby Pfeil
Mike Phillips
Rich Puig
Mario Ramirez
Lenny Randle
Tommie Reynolds
Amado Samuel
Ted Schreiber
Charley Smith
Roy Staiger
John Stearns
John Stephenson
Frank Thomas
Joe Torre
Alex Trevino
Bobby Valentine
Al Weis
Joel Youngblood
Don Zimmer

---

*Played 3rd base for the Mets after Brooks became the regular in 1981.

No Room for Error

According to AL veteran umpire Nestor Chylak, "Umpiring is the only job in the world where you are expected to be perfect when you are hired and then improve as time goes by."

5.

THE GOOD, THE BAD, AND THE UGLY

Questions

NO JOY IN MUDVILLE

632. *Who threw Roger Maris his 61st home run pitch?*

633. *What player committed the most errors in one season?*

634. *What pitcher walked the most batters in one inning?*

635. *Who pulled off an unassisted triple play and was traded three days later after he struck out six straight times?*

636. *What player committed the most errors in one game?*

637. *What player committed the most errors on one play?*

638. *Whose failure to touch 2nd base cost his team a pennant?*

639. *What Boston Red Sox shortstop held the ball as if snakebit while Enos Slaughter scored all the way from 1st base on a single with the winning run as St. Louis won the deciding game of the 1946 World series?*

Answers

NO JOY IN MUDVILLE

632. Boston right-hander Tracy Stallard, 10/1/61, at Yankee Stadium.

633. Joseph Sullivan, shortstop for Washington in 1893, was guilty of 106 errors.

634. William "Dolly" Gray, Washington, walked eight Chicago batters in the first inning on 8/20/09. Seven of those walks were successive, setting another record.

635. Ron Hansen, Washington Senators, traded to Chicago (AL), 8/3/68.

636. Andy Leonard, Boston 2nd baseman, committed 9 errors on 6/14/1876.

637. Mike Grady, Philadelphia, made 3 errors on one batted ball in 1895.

638. Fred Merkle, 9/23/08. His failure to advance from 1st to 2nd on a base hit nullified a run. As the jubilant crowd at the Polo Grounds stormed the field, the Chicago fielders somehow got the ball to 2nd base and forced out Merkle, ending the inning. The two teams finished tied for the pennant, and the Giants lost in a one-game playoff, thus earning Merkle the nickname "Bonehead."

639. Johnny Pesky, 10/15/46.

Questions

640. *What was the only team to lose a tripleheader?*

641. *What three players have hit into 4 double plays in one game?*

642. *What pitcher gave up the most home runs in one season?*

643. *What player hit into the most triple plays in his career?*

644. *What team holds the record for the most errors in one season?*

645. *Who holds the record for uncorking the most wild pitches in a game?*

646. *By record, what was absolutely, positively, the worst team ever?*

Answers

640. The Brooklyn Dodgers dropped three games. to Pittsburgh on 6/2/03. The last two teams to play a tripleheader were the Reds and Pirates at Forbes Field, 10/2/20.

641. Goose Goslin, Detroit, 4/28/34
Mike Kreevich, Chicago White Sox, 8/4/39
Joe Torre, NY Mets, 7/21/75.

642. Robin Roberts threw 46 gopher balls for Philadelphia in 1956.

643. Brooks Robinson, 4.

644. The 1886 Washington club made 867 errors in 122 games. The AL record is held by the 1901 Detroit Tigers who made 425 bobbles in 136 games.

645. On 7/22/1876, John J. Ryan of Louisville threw 10 away.

646. The 1899 Cleveland Spiders, 20-134. Six times during the season they lost 11 or more games in succession including one streak of 24 straight losses which is the major league record. Only once did they win two in a row. They finished the season 80 games behind the pennant-winning Brooklyn Dodgers. Their leading pitcher was Jim Hughey, who was 4-30!

Questions

647. *What Dartmouth bonus baby pitched for five last-place teams in eight seasons?*

648. *Who holds the record for going hitless in the most at bats in one season?*

649. *The Yankees hold many records. One of the more obscure is for having stranded the most runners in a 9-inning game. How many?*

650. *What was the only team to lose consecutive pennants in the last inning of the last game of the season?*

651. *What two pitchers share the dubious distinction of surrendering four grand slams in a season?*

652. *What major league catcher hit into a triple play in his last career at bat?*

653. *What pitcher gave up the most gopher balls in his career?*

654. *What pitcher balked the most times in one game?*

655. *What was the most lopsided score of a big league game?*

Answers

647. Pete Broberg, 1971-78.

648. Bob Buhl, Chicago Cubs pitcher, went 0 for 70 in 1962.

649. 20, 9/21/56.

650. The Brooklyn Dodgers, 1950 and 1951, to Philadelphia and New York, respectively.

651. Ray Narleski, Cleveland, 1949, and Tug McGraw, Philadelphia, 1979.

652. Joe Pignatano, New York Mets, 1962. What a way to go!

653. Robin Roberts, 502, in 19 seasons.

654. Bob Shaw, Milwaukee, 5, 5/4/63, including 3 in one inning.

655. Cap Anson's Chicago Colts beat the Louisville Colonels 36-7 on 6/29/1887.

Questions

656. What player stranded the most runners in one game?

657. What pitcher holds the record for consecutive losses to the same team?

658. What team lost the most consecutive games to another team?

659. What pitcher holds the record for consecutive losses?

660. What club had a team batting average of .315 and finished dead last!?

661. What player holds the record for the most times leading the league in double plays grounded into?

662. What pitcher tied the record for walks in his very first game?

663. What two pitchers, each with at least 300 career wins, share the record for the most wild pitches in an inning?

664. What pitcher was rocked for the most runs in one inning?

Answers

656. Glenn Beckert, Chicago Cubs, 12, 9/16/72. Fortunately for Beckert, the Cubs beat the Mets 18-5.

657. Don Sutton lost 13 in a row to the Chicago Cubs from 4/23/66 to 7/24/69. All 13 of those decisions came at the start of the Dodger righty's career.

658. From 5/10/69 through 8/2/70, Kansas City lost 23 straight to Baltimore.

659. Clifton Curtis, Boston Braves, dropped 23 straight decisions from 6/13/10 through 5/22/11.

660. The 1930 Philadelphia Phillies. With a 52-102 record, they finished 40 games out of first. Their mound staff compiled a whopping 6.71 ERA.

661. Ernie Lombardi, 4.

662. Bruno Haas, 16, Philadelphia Athletics, 6/23/15. He shares the mark with three others.

663. Walter Johnson, Washington, 9/21/14, and Phil Niekro, Atlanta, 8/4/79. Each uncorked 4 wild pitches.

664. Tony Mullane, Baltimore, gave up 16 1st-inning runs on 6/18/1894.

Questions

665. Who is the only pitcher to have given up four consecutive home runs?

666. What pitcher took the biggest nosedive in victories from one year to the next?

667. What pitcher lost the most games at the start of his career?

668. Who gave up Pete Rose's record-breaking 4,192nd base hit?

Answers

665. On 7/31/63, Los Angeles Angels' hurler Paul Foy-tack gave up homers to Cleveland batters Woody Held, Pedro Ramos, Tito Francona, and Larry Brown.

666. Al Spalding won 46 games for Chicago in 1876. The next season he won the grand total of one!

667. Terry Felton, 16, Minnesota, 1980-82. He never won a game in the majors.

668. Eric Show, San Diego, 9/11/85. It was a slicing single to left-center off the right-handed Show. The hit came on a 2-1 pitch with one out in the bottom of the first inning at Cincinnati's Riverfront Stadium. According to home plate umpire Lee Weyer, who also worked 3rd base the night Hank Aaron broke Babe Ruth's career home run record, the delivery was a belt-high slider.

Questions

BASEBALL'S FUNNY BONE

669. *What screwball once stole 1st base from 2nd base?*

670. *What player ran the bases backwards after hitting his 100th career homer?*

671. *This player, notorious for hitting foul balls, hit a spectator with a foul. Then, while still at bat, this former Phillie hit yet another foul ball that struck the same fan while he was being removed on a stretcher. Who was he?*

672. *What unusual mannerism did Lew Burdette possess?*

673. *What pitcher threw so hard that his hat came off an unofficial record 38 times in a single World Series game?*

674. *What former manager once lost 18 straight games as a pitcher for the New York Mets?*

675. *This catcher beat up Ty Cobb and later in his career as a Dodger coach, drove nails into the clubhouse floor at Ebbets Field with his fists. Who was he?*

Answers

BASEBALL'S FUNNY BONE

669. Germany Schaefer, Detroit. He promptly restole 2nd base!

670. Jimmy Piersall, with the NY Mets in 1963. Piersall was the same flake who watered down home plate with a water pistol.

671. Richie Ashburn.

672. He ran from the dugout to the batter's box each time up.

673. New York Yankee Jim Bouton.

674. Roger Craig, 1963. After changing the numeral on his jersey to #13, he won!

675. Charlie Schmidt.

Questions

676. *What Texas Ranger appeared on the 1979 Topps bubble gum card as a member of the Toronto Blue Jays?*

677. *What was the name of Bill Veeck's pinch-hitting midget?*

678. *What zany player was a bare knuckle boxer, swallowed lighted cigarettes, removed tattoos with razor blades, pulled his own teeth with a pair of pliers, slurped beer through a straw stuck up his nose, and opened beer bottles for his teammates with his eye sockets?*

679. *What flake shined his shoes in the on-deck circle in the 15th inning with the bases loaded, set off firecrackers in the dugout, and hit tennis balls in the clubhouse runway in the middle of a game?*

Answers

676. Bump Wills.

677. Eddie Gaedel, 8/19/51. The 3'7" Gaedel took his toy bat to the plate to pinch-hit for Frank Saucier. With a strike zone measured at 1½ inches when Gaedel crouched, frustrated Detroit pitcher Bob Cain threw four straight balls to catcher Bob Swift. The home plate umpire, Ed Hurley, told Gaedel to take his base. Number 1/8 walked to 1st base where he was replaced by Jim Delsing. After the incident, AL president Will Harridge said, "There will be no more of that, boys."

678. Joe Charboneau.

679. Jay Johnstone.

Questions

THE TROPHY CASE

680. *Who was the only pitcher to win a Cy Young Award while hurling for a last-place team?*

681. *What is the Ford C. Frick Award?*

682. *Who are the five relievers to have won the Cy Young Award?*

683. *Who sponsors the "Relief Man of the Year" award?*

684. *Who was the only pitcher to win the Cy Young Award three times unanimously?*

685. *What was the original Most Valuable Player award called?*

686. *Who was the first NL player to be chosen MVP unanimously?*

687. *Who was the youngest player to win the MVP Award?*

688. *What is the Aqua Velva Cup Award?*

Answers

THE TROPHY CASE

680. Steve Carlton, Philadelphia, 1972. He led the NL in starts, complete games, innings pitched, wins, ERA, and strikeouts.

681. Established on 8/7/78 at Cooperstown, it is given for baseball broadcasting excellence. Its first recipients were Mel Allen and Red Barber.

682.
Mike Marshall	1974 Los Angeles Dodgers
Sparky Lyle	1977 New York Yankees
Bruce Sutter	1979 Chicago Cubs
Rollie Fingers	1981 Milwaukee Brewers
Willie Hernandez	1984 Detroit Tigers.

683. Warner-Lambert Company, maker of Rolaids.

684. Sandy Koufax, Los Angeles, 1963, 1965, and 1966.

685. The Chalmers Award. In 1911 this award was named after a popular automobile of that era. The award was given only four years.

686. Orlando Cepeda, St. Louis, 1967. Mike Schmidt for Philadelphia in 1980 was the only other man to be so honored.

687. Vida Blue, Oakland, was 22 years and 5 months when he won the MVP in 1971.

688. First presented in 1979, it is awarded to the major league player with the season's longest hitting streak.

Questions

689. What award is listed under "miscellaneous awards" in the AL Redbook and isn't even listed in the Official Baseball Guide?

690. Who was the youngest man to win both the Cy Young and the MVP awards?

691. Who is the only player to win both the Rookie of the Year and the MVP awards in the same season?

692. Who is the only player to win the MVP Award in the World Series and league championship series, as well as for the regular season?

693. Who was the only player to win the Rookie of the Year, the Cy Young, and the MVP awards in his career?

694. Who was the major leagues' first black MVP?

695. What seven pitchers won both the Cy Young Award and the MVP Award in the same season?

696. What was the only season when the MVPs from each league were pitchers?

697. What was the only season when both Cy Young winners were left-handers?

Answers

689. Comeback Player of the Year.

690. Vida Blue, Oakland, 1971, age 22.

691. Fred Lynn, Boston Red Sox, 1975.

692. Willie Stargell, Pittsburgh, 1979. The award for the regular season was shared with St. Louis' Keith Hernandez, the first time the MVP voting resulted in a tie.

693. Don Newcombe.

694. Jackie Robinson, Brooklyn, 1949. The first black AL MVP was Elston Howard of New York in 1963.

695.

Don Newcombe	1956	Brooklyn Dodgers
Sandy Koufax	1963	Los Angeles Dodgers
Bob Gibson	1968	St. Louis Cardinals
Denny McLain	1968	Detroit Tigers
Vida Blue	1971	Oakland A's
Rollie Fingers	1981	Milwaukee Brewers
Willie Hernandez	1984	Detroit Tigers.

696. 1968. St. Louis' Bob Gibson and Detroit's Denny McLain, both right-handers.

697. 1977. Steve Carlton of Philadelphia (NL) and Sparky Lyle of New York (AL).

Questions

698. Who is the only hurler to win the Fireman of the Year Award five times?

699. Who was the first rookie to win the Cy Young Award?

700. Who was the only American League player to win the MVP while playing for a fourth-place team?

701. Since the MVP Award was established in 1931, how many players who batted over .400 have won the honor?

702. Who is the only pitcher to win the Cy Young Award four times?

703. When was the first year that 3rd basemen won both the NL and the AL MVP awards?

704. The fielding positions of the nine men who have won back-to-back MVPs, ironically enough, would fill each of the nine defensive positions on the diamond. Who are these players and at what position did they win their MVPs?

705. Who are the only three relief pitchers to win the MVP Award?

Answers

698. Dan Quisenberry, 1980, 1982-85, all with Kansas City.

699. Fernando Valenzuela, Los Angeles, 1981.

700. Bobby Shantz, Philadelphia Athletics, 1952.

701. None.

702. Steve Carlton, 1972, 1977, 1980, and 1982, all with Philadelphia.

703. 1964. Ken Boyer, St. Louis (NL), and Brooks Robinson, Baltimore (AL). 3rd basemen have captured both MVPs in only one other year, 19890, when Mike Schmidt of Philadelphia (NL) and George Brett of Kansas City (AL) were honored.

704.

1B	Jimmie Foxx	1932-33	Philadelphia (AL)
2B	Joe Morgan	1975-76	Cincinnati (NL)
SS	Ernie Banks	1958-59	Chicago (NL)
3B	Mike Schmidt	1980-81	Philadelphia (NL)
OF	Dale Murphy	1982-83	Atlanta (NL)
OF	Mickey Mantle	1956-57	New York (AL)
OF	Roger Maris	1960-61	New York (AL)
C	Yogi Berra	1954-55	New York (AL)
P	Hal Newhouser	1944-45	Detroit (AL).

705. Jim Konstanty, Philadelphia (NL), 1950, Rollie Fingers, Milwaukee (AL), 1981, and Willie Hernandez, Detroit (AL), 1984.

Questions

OCCUPATIONAL HAZARDS

706. What pitcher was involved in the beaning of Tony Conigliaro?

707. What batter struck Cleveland ace Herb Score in the face with a line drive?

708. What shortstop had his career shortened by frozen feet which he acquired in World War II's "Battle of the Bulge"?

709. Who was the master of using the old baggy uniform as a means of getting hit by the pitch?

710. What two pitchers hit the first three batters they faced in a game?

711. What outfielder had but one arm?

712. Who was the only pitcher to be ejected from a game and suspended for the season for throwing a brushback pitch?

713. What was sometimes used as an outfield boundary in the early days of the major leagues?

714. What batter ended Red Ruffing's career with a line drive off his right kneecap?

Answers

OCCUPATIONAL HAZARDS

706. Jack Hamilton, California, 8/18/67.

707. Gil McDougald of the Yankees, 5/7/57.

708. Cecil Travis, Washington Senators, 1933-47.

709. Eddie Yost, 1944-62.

710. Emerson Hawley, St. Louis, 7/4/1894; Dock Ellis, Pittsburgh, duplicated the feat eighty years later when he plunked Cincy batters Pete Rose, Joe Morgan, and Dan Driessen on 5/1/74.

711. Pete Gray, St. Louis Browns, 1945.

712. Dave Danforth, St. Louis Browns, 1923.

713. Barbed wire.

714. Hank Majeski, Philadelphia Athletics, 1947.

Questions

715. *What catcher was refused reentry to the major leagues after jumping to the Mexican League?*

716. *What pitcher hit the most batters in one season?*

717. *What pitcher holds the record for hitting the most batters in his career?*

718. *Billy Martin was involved in four one-punch ballpark decisions during his baseball career to date. Who were the four players Billy belted?*

719. *What California Angel was shot to death by an assailant who mistook him for another man?*

720. *In 1965 a Giant pitcher struck a Dodger catcher over the head with a bat. For this action he was fined $1,750 and suspended for three pitching turns. Who were the principals involved?*

721. *Who hit Dizzy Dean with a line drive that hastened the end of Dean's career?*

722. *What strange circumstances surrounded Ray Chapman on 8/16/20, the day he was beaned and killed by a pitch?*

Answers

715. Mickey Owen, Brooklyn, 1946.

716. Joe McGinnity hit 41 batters while pitching for Brooklyn in 1900.

717. Walter Johnson, 206.

718. Matt Batts, Jim Piersall, Clint Courtney, and Jim Brewer. His fight as manager of Minnesota in 1969 with his own pitcher, Dave Boswell, took two crunching punches.

719. Lyman Bostock, 1978.

720. Juan Marichal of the Giants and John Roseboro of the Dodgers. Punishment was administered by NL president Warren Giles.

721. Earl Averill, in the 1937 All-Star Game.

722. Chapman was batting second in the lineup. He had 2 hits, both two-base hits. He had scored 2 runs and had stolen 2 bases. In the field he had 2 putouts. 2 assists, and had committed 2 errors. The Cleveland shortstop was hit by 2 pitches. The second pitch was the one he never saw. The ball struck him with such force in the temple that it rolled down to 3rd base. The Yankee pitcher that day, Carl Mays, was, like Chapman, a native of Kentucky.

Questions

723. Who was the slugging AL 1st baseman whose turbulent career was cut short by migraine headaches?

724. What Pirate pitcher was struck on the left leg by the ball and on the right leg by the bat of Jay Johnstone of the Padres?

725. What NL Rookie of the Year was killed in the crash of a private plane near Provo, Utah, in 1965?

726. What shortstop returned to play after losing the tips of the fingers on his throwing hand in an accident?

727. What player was hit by pitches most often in his career?

728. Who were the only two players hit by a pitch twice in one inning?

Answers

723. Hal Trosky. With Cleveland from 1933 to 1941 and Chicago in 1944 and 1946, Trosky hit 228 home runs and compiled a .302 average.

724. Bruce Kison.

725. Kenny Hubbs, 1962 Rookie of the Year 2nd baseman with Chicago.

726. Roger Metzger, San Francisco, 1980.

727. Ron Hunt, 243 times, including a single-season high of 50 in 1971 while with Montreal.

728. Willard Schmidt, Cincinnati, 4/26/59, and Frank Thomas, NY Mets, 4/29/62.

Questions

729. How did the saying "Say it ain't so, Joe" originate?

730. What pitcher was ordered to change into a different uniform during a game?

731. What player drew a $5,000 fine from the AL president for "contemptuous conduct toward the paying customers and the press"?

732. Who were the eight players involved in the infamous Black Sox Scandal of 1919?

733. What three Hall of Famers were members of the Ku Klux Klan?

734. What other scandal occurred the same year as the Black Sox Scandal?

Answers

QUIET, PLEASE!

729. "Shoeless" Joe Jackson's involvement with the Black Sox Scandal of 1919-20 prompted a child with tear-filled eyes to beg the Chicago star, "Say it ain't so, Joe."

730. Gaylord Perry. His being suspected of greasing the ball prompted this action by the umpires.

731. "Terrible Ted" Williams.

732. Ed Cicotte, Lefty Williams, Joe Jackson, Buck Weaver, Chick Gandil, Swede Risberg, Happy Felsch, and Fred McMullin. All were cleared of the charge of throwing the World Series by a federal grand jury but were barred from organized baseball for life.

733. Gabby Street, Rogers Hornsby, and Tris Speaker. It was rumored that Ty Cobb was a member of the KKK, but it was never confirmed.

734. Almost covered up by the Black Sox Scandal was a purported conspiracy to throw a game between Detroit and Cleveland. It came to light in 1926 and resulted in commissioner Landis banishing Ty Cobb and Tris Speaker from their respective teams. Cobb signed with the A's and Speaker with the Senators.

Questions

735. *A Hall of Fame player had to stay out of Ohio for a year-and-a-half to avoid arrest for knifing a Negro waiter in Cleveland. Who was he?*

736. *How many times was Alex Johnson fined by the California Angels in 1971?*

737. *What Hall of Famer suffered from venereal disease?*

738. *What major league pitcher had to be locked in his hotel room the night before he pitched a pennant-winning game?*

739. *What former Baltimore player's brother was arrested outside of Baltimore's Memorial Stadium for scalping World Series tickets and possession of hashish?*

740. *What player or manager received baseball's longest suspension that did not involve an umpire?*

741. *What two Yankees swapped wives in 1973?*

Answers

735. Ty Cobb.

736. 29. He never paid a one. He took his case to arbitration pleading emotional illness.

737. Casey Stengel, 1914-15.

738. Jack Jakucki, 1944 St. Louis Browns, by his manager Luke Sewell. Jakucki proceeded to beat the Yankees to win the only Brown pennant on the last day of the season.

739. John Garcia, 24-year-old brother of Kiko Garcia, 1979.

740. Denny McLain was suspended for the last half of 1970 for alleged gambling. The longest provoked suspension involving an umpire was of Bill Madlock, who on 5/1/80, allegedly pushed his glove into the face of umpire Jerry Crawford. The suspension lasted 15 days (11 games) and cost the Pirate 3rd baseman $5,000.

741. Fritz Peterson and Mike Kekich.

Questions

COOPERSTOWN

742. Who is the only man elected to the baseball, football, and collegiate football halls of fame?

743. Who are the two Jewish members of the Hall of Fame?

744. Who are the only two Hall of Fame pitchers to lose more games than they won?

745. Who is the only Hall of Fame member to hit a homer in his first at bat?

746. What player hit a Jack Fisher fastball for his 521st homer in his last at bat in the majors?

747. What man enshrined at Cooperstown won 158 games on the mound and stroked 2,122 hits?

748. Who are the five umpires in the Hall of Fame?

749. Who were the first five players inducted into the Hall of Fame?

750. What player received the most votes on his induction into the Hall of Fame?

751. What Hall of Famer signed a major league contract for a dollar?

Answers

COOPERSTOWN

742. Cal Hubbard.

743. Hank Greenberg and Sandy Koufax.

744. Satchel Paige was 28-31 in the major leagues but was inducted for his career in the Negro leagues. William "Candy" Cummings was 21-22 lifetime but made it to Cooperstown on the premise that he was the inventor of the curve ball.

745. Earl Averill, Cleveland, 4/16/29, homered off Detroit's Earl Whitehill.

746. Ted Williams.

747. John "Monte" Ward, Chicago, 1878-94. On 6/17/1880, he pitched a perfect game for Providence over Buffalo 5-0.

748. Bill Klem, Tom Connolly, Billy Evans, Jocko Conlon, and Cal Hubbard.

749. Babe Ruth, Ty Cobb, Christy Mathewson, Walter Johnson, and Honus Wagner, all inducted in 1936.

750. Willie Mays received 409 votes when he was inducted in 1979.

751. Bob Feller, Cleveland. This signing started the phrase, "A ball and a buck."

Questions

752. What three non-pitching members of the Hall of Fame never once hit .300 in their careers?

753. Who are the only two men honored in the Hall of Fame who never had a thing to do with major league baseball?

754. What two Hall of Famers were inducted via special waiver of the five-year waiting period normally required after a player's final year of pro ball?

755. What two Hall of Famers teamed up to broadcast Detroit Tiger ball games?

Answers

752. Shortstop Rabbit Maranville, catcher Ray Schalk, and infielder Harmon Killebrew.

753. Bud Abbott and Lou Costello. Found in Cooperstown is a copy of their "Who's on first?" routine.

754. Lou Gehrig, 1939, and Roberto Clemente, 1973. Each received a special waiver because of their untimely deaths.

755. Al Kaline and George Kell.

Sidelights

FOR THE GOOD, THE BAD, AND THE UGLY

Statistics Are for Losers

Joe Bauman owns the minor league record for home runs and RBIs in a single season. He cracked 72 homers and drove in 224 runs at Roswell, New Mexico, in 1954. He also batted .400 on the nose. Unfortunately for Bauman, he never earned a spot on a major league roster.

A New Anthem

On May 9, 1980, in Arlington Stadium, home of the Texas Rangers, the public address announcer requested that the fans rise for the playing of the national anthem. However, the engineer pushed the wrong button and the crowd heard "CHARGE!"

The Ryan Award

California Angels general manager Harry Dalton made the statement to the 1978 press, "They should give Cy Young the Nolan Ryan Award!" Despite all the strikeouts that Ryan has totaled up over the years, Ryan has never won the Cy Young Award.

September Series

The earliest date a World Series game has ever been played was on September 5. This occurred in 1918 because of wartime regulations which halted the regular season on Labor Day. The Boston Red Sox and Chicago Cubs finished the six-game series (won by Boston 4-2) on September 11.

The Biter

Former Cincinnati pitcher Pedro Borbon certainly has an unusual appetite. He once bit a piece out of a New York Met cap when he discovered he had mistakenly put it on his head. He later bit a bartender on the chest!

What a Series They Would Have Had

The following is a list of Hall of Famers who never played in a World Series:

Luke Appling
Ernie Banks
Harry Heilman
George Kell
Ralph Kiner
Ted Lyons
George Sisler

Many other Hall of Famers never played in the World Series simply because they played part or all of their careers before the World Series began in 1903, or because they played in the Negro leagues.

6.

NAME, RANK,
AND SERIAL NUMBER

Questions

THE BOOK OF NUMBERS

756. *What number did Babe Ruth wear on his uniform when he hit his 60th home run on September 30, 1927?*

757. *What player had his minor league uniform number retired when he advanced to the majors?*

758. *Who are the only two men to have their uniforms retired by two teams?*

759. *What was the first team to carry names on uniforms and in what year?*

760. *What uniform number has been retired most often?*

Answers

THE BOOK OF NUMBERS

756. None! Numbers were not added to Yankee uniforms until 1929. Cleveland was the first team that adopted the practice of wearing numbers, 6/26/16. The 1888 Cincinnati Redlegs wore numbers on their sleeves for a time but stopped the idea because the players deemed it too impersonal.

757. Johnny Bench had his uniform number #19 retired from the Peninsula Grays of the Class AA Carolina League in 1967. Ten years later, however, it was reissued to another player. In the NL, Bench wore #5 for Cincinnati.

758. Hank Aaron's #44 by the Atlanta Braves and the Milwaukee Brewers, and Casey Stengel's #37 by the New York Yankees and the New York Mets.

759. The 1960 Chicago White Sox.

760. Number 4. Luke Appling, White Sox; Lou Gehrig, Yankees; Mel Ott, Giants; Duke Snider, Dodgers; Earl Weaver, Orioles. Weaver's number has been temporarily unretired since he returned to manage Baltimore in 1985.

Questions

THE NAMES OF THE GAME

761. What player owns the longest name in major league history?

762. What five players formed the nucleus of the original "Murderers' Row" for the NY Yankees?

763. What players made up the "$100,000 infield"?

764. What caused "The Miracle of Coogan's Bluff"?

765. What team had the battle cry "Ya gotta believe"?

766. Who was "The Ancient Mariner"?

767. Who gave Yankee Stadium the nickname "The House That Ruth Built"?

768. What pitcher is known as "The Man with the Bionic Arm"?

Answers

THE NAMES OF THE GAME

761. Alan Edward Mitchell George Patrick Henry "Dirty Al" Gallagher, 1970-73.

762. Wally Pipp, Babe Ruth, Roger Peckinpaugh, Bob Meusel, and Frank "Home Run" Baker were the feared hitters in the 1921 Yankee lineup.

763. 1B Stuffy McInnis SS Jack Barry
     2B Eddie Collins   3B Frank "Home Run" Baker

    The four were members of the 1911-14 Philadelphia Athletics.

764. Bobby Thomson's pennant-winning home run into the left field porch at the Polo Grounds on October 3, 1951.

765. The 1973 NL champion New York Mets. The phrase was coined by Met reliever Tug McGraw.

766. Diego Segui, at age 39, started the Seattle Mariners first game ever in 1977. Segui was also a member of the previous team in Seattle, the 1969 Pilots.

767. Sportswriter Fred Lieb.

768. Tommy John. Corrective surgery to his left arm in 1975 renewed his career.

Questions

769. *What pitcher was called "Rufus the Red"?*

770. *Who were the catchers for the 1934 St. Louis Cardinals "Gas House Gang"?*

771. *Where was "Greenberg Gardens" located?*

772. *What was "Pasquel's Raid"?*

773. *Who were referred to as the major leagues' "Odd Couple"?*

774. *Who was dubbed baseball's "Mad Trader"?*

775. *Where was "Duffy's Cliff"?*

776. *What Hall of Fame enshrinee was known as "The Father of Baseball"?*

777. *Who was the first major leaguer to carry the nickname "Home Run"?*

Answers

769. Charles "Red" Ruffing, 1924-46. He performed his pitching magic despite losing four toes on his left foot that were severed in a mining accident at the age of 13.

770. Bill DeLancey and Virgil "Spud" Davis.

771. Beyond the left field fence at Pittsburgh's Forbes Field in 1947.

772. Mexico's Pasquel brothers tried to use their wealth to lure American players south of the border in 1946.

773. Washington manager Ted Williams and his pitcher Denny McLain in 1971.

774. Frank Lane.

775. Before the erection of the "Green Monster" at Fenway Park in Boston, the left field terrain rose to 8 feet. Duffy Lewis played the hazard so well that it became known as "Duffy's Cliff."

776. Alexander Cartwright. He is given credit for having drawn up the first set of baseball rules and having organized the first team, the Knickerbockers, in 1845.

777. Charlie Duffee, 1889-93.

Questions

778. Where is "Death Valley" located in the big leagues?

779. From what team did the NY Mets derive their nickname?

780. Who was known as "The Giant Killer"?

781. Who were known as the "Bones Battery"?

782. What did the Dodgers have to dodge to get their beloved nickname?

783. What did Babe Ruth name his bats?

784. Who were known as "The Daffiness Boys"?

785. Who were "The Heavenly Twins"?

786. Where is "The Launching Pad"?

787. Who was known as "Big Six"?

788. Who was known as "the doctor of sick ball games"?

Answers

778. Yankee Stadium's left-center field, which stretches 411 feet from home plate.

779. From the old American Association's New York Metropolitans.

780. Harry Coveleski, on the strength of his beating the Giants three times in one week for the Phillies in 1908.

781. Frank Gilmore and catcher Connie Mack, Washington, 1886. In the minor leagues at Hartford, the same duo was known as the "Shadow Battery."

782. The trolley cars of Brooklyn. The club has also been known as the Robins and the Bridegrooms.

783. "Black Betsy."

784. The 1925 Brooklyn Robins.

785. Hall of Fame members Tom McCarthy and Hugh Duffy, Boston, 1892.

786. Atlanta-Fulton County Stadium in Atlanta, Georgia.

787. Christy Mathewson. He acquired the moniker from admiring fans who referred to New York City's fastest horse and fire engine at that time.

788. Otis "Doc" Crandall, 1908-18.

Questions

789. What first baseman has been dubbed "The Human Rain Delay"?

790. What team was known as "Five O'clock Lightning?"

791. Who was the "Pilot Light" of the St. Louis Cardinals' "Gas House Gang"?

792. What four players made up "The Diaper Squad"?

793. From 1944 through 1945 the NL Philadelphia franchise was not known as the Phillies. What were they called?

794. The Chicago NL franchise has been known by 18 different nicknames. What are they?

795. Who were "The Gold Dust Twins"?

Answers

789. Mike Hargrove, AL 1st baseman, 1974- . He has been timed at 15 seconds to enter the batter's box.

790. The 1927 NY Yankees, who usually finished their games by five o'clock in the afternoon. In that year, the Bronx Bombers had three of the top four pitchers in ERA!

791. Frankie Frisch.

792. The 1960 Baltimore Oriole starters Milt Pappas, Steve Barber, Jerry Walker, and Chuck Estrada. All were 21 years old.

793. The Blue Jays.

794. The White Stockings, the Colts, The Black Stockings, the Ex-Colts, the Rainmakers, the Orphans, the Cowboys, the Rough Riders, the Desert Rangers, the Pennants, the Recruits, the Zephyrs, the Nationals, the Fourth Nationals, the Third Nationals, the Spuds, and the Trojans. The owners finally settled on "Cubs" in 1908. The number of nicknames establishes a record.

795. New York Yankee pitchers Ron Davis and Goose Gossage were so named by their manager in 1981, Bob Lemon.

Questions

NEW KID ON THE BLOCK

796. What are the prerequisites for Rookie of the Year consideration?

797. Who holds the rookie record for highest batting average?

798. What player holds the record for most hits as a rookie?

799. Who holds the rookie record for doubles?

800. Who holds the rookie record for triples?

801. What two men share the record for home runs as a rookie?

802. What rookie had the most RBIs in his freshman year?

803. Who holds the rookie record for runs scored?

804. What rookie walked the most times in his first year?

805. What rookie struck out the most times in his first year?

Answers

NEW KID ON THE BLOCK

796. A player must not have had more than 130 at bats or 50 innings pitched in the major leagues during a previous season or seasons, nor must he have spent more than 45 days on a major league roster during the 25-player limit (excluding time in the military service).

797. George Watkins, St. Louis Cardinals, hit .373 in 119 games in 1930. The AL high was set in 1929 by the Detroit Tigers' Dale Alexander with .343.

798. Lloyd Waner, Pittsburgh, 223, 1927.

799. John Frederick, Brooklyn, 52, 1929.

800. Paul Waner, Pittsburgh, 22, 1926.

801. The record is jointly held by Wally Berger of the 1930 Boston Braves and Frank Robinson of the 1956 Cincinnati Reds. Each man hit 38.

802. Ted Williams, Boston Red Sox, plated 145 runners in 1939.

803. Lloyd Waner, Pittsburgh, 133, 1927.

804. Ted Williams, Boston Red Sox, walked 107 times in 1939.

805. Juan Samuel, 168, Philadelphia, 1984.

Questions

806. What rookie stole the most bases in his initial season?

807. What pitcher had the best ERA as a rookie?

808. What pitcher holds the rookie record for wins?

809. What pitcher struck out the most batters as a rookie?

810. Who was the oldest rookie ever?

811. Who holds the record for consecutive hits at the start of his career?

812. What rookie pitcher shut out the Yankees three times in his first four days in the big leagues?

813. What two men hit grand slams in their first major league games?

814. What pitcher holds the rookie record for shutouts?

815. What pitcher holds the rookie record for strikeouts in one game?

816. Who was the first rookie to win a batting crown?

Answers

806. Vince Coleman, 110, St. Louis, 1985.

807. Mark Fidrych posted a 2.34 ERA with Detroit in 1976.

808. Al Spalding won 47 for Chicago in 1876.

809. Dwight Gooden fanned 276 batters for the New York Mets in 1984.

810. Satchel Paige. He was 42 when he finally made the bigs in 1948 with Cleveland.

811. Ted Cox got six straight hits for Boston in 1977.

812. Walter Johnson, Washington, 1907, at the tender age of 19.

813. Bill Duggleby, Philadelphia, 4/4/1898, and Bobby Bonds, San Francisco, 6/25/68.

814. George Bradley, 16 with St. Louis in 1876. The AL record was set by Babe Ruth with 9 for Boston in 1916.

815. Montreal's Bill Gullickson fanned 18 Cubs on 9/10/80.

816. Abner Dalrymple, Milwaukee, 1878, .356.

Questions

817. What two players struck five hits in their first big league games?

818. Who was the first rookie to collect 200 hits?

819. What rookie pitcher completed the most games in his first year?

820. What club has had the most Rookies of the Year and who are they?

821. What two pitchers share the rookie record for appearances?

Answers

817. Fred Clarke, Louisville, 6/30/1894, and Cecil Travis, Washington, 5/16/33.

818. Jimmy Williams, rapped 219 hits for Pittsburgh in 1899.

819. James Devlin completed *all* 67 games he started for Louisville in 1876. The AL record is held by Roscoe Miller who completed 36 of 38 games for Detroit in 1901.

820. The Brooklyn/Los Angeles Dodgers have had 11 Rookies of the Year. They are:

Jackie Robinson	1947
Don Newcombe	1949
Joe Black	1952
Jim Gilliam	1953
Frank Howard	1960
Jim Lefebvre	1965
Ted Sizemore	1969
Rick Sutcliffe	1979
Steve Howe	1980
Fernando Valenzuela	1981
Steve Sax	1982.

821. Ed Vande Berg appeared in 78 games for Seattle in 1982. Tim Burke tied the mark with Montreal in 1985.

Questions

ALL IN THE FAMILY

822. *What famous tennis star is pitcher Randy Moffitt's sister?*

823. *What was the only brother battery in the All-Star Game?*

824. *Who are the two sets of brothers in the Hall of Fame?*

825. *What was the last brother battery in the big leagues?*

826. *Which famous National Football League running back is the cousin of Ernie Banks?*

827. *What two brothers hit the most home runs between them?*

828. *His sister once held the Olympic record for the hurdles. His brother was drafted by the NFL Kansas City Chiefs. Who was this major leaguer?*

829. *What two sets of brothers won 20 games each in the same season?*

830. *What three brothers combined to win 386 major league games?*

Answers

ALL IN THE FAMILY

822. Billie Jean King.

823. Mort and Walker Cooper, St. Louis (NL), 1942.

824. Paul and Lloyd Waner, and George and Harry Wright.

825. Larry and Norm Sherry, Los Angeles, 1962.

826. O. J. Simpson.

827. The Aarons. Hank hit 755 and Tommie hit 13 for a total of 768.

828. Bobby Bonds.

829. Jim and Gaylord Perry in 1970 were the first brothers to accomplish this. Older brother Jim threw for Minnesota and Gaylord hurled for San Francisco. They were followed by Joe and Phil Niekro who turned the trick in 1979. Phil played for Atlanta while little brother Joe pitched for Houston.

830. John (327), Arthur (39), and Walter (20) Clarkson all pitched in the 1800s.

Questions

831. Who are the only brothers to pitch no-hitters in the big leagues?

832. Who are the only two sets of brothers that averaged over .300 in their careers of ten or more years?

833. Who are the only brothers to hit consecutive home runs?

834. What former batting champion had a brother Ron who was a star runner with the NFL NY Giants?

835. Who are the four father/son combinations that appeared in the World Series in their own eras?

836. What big league infielder had a brother who played for the NFL Balitmore Colts?

837. Tony of the Dodgers and Al of the Giants were brothers. In the same game in 1935 they both hit home runs. However it was brother Al's first major league home run. What was their last name?

Answers

831. The Forsch brothers. Bob did it first on 4/12/78 for St. Louis over the Phillies, 5-0. Brother Ken of Houston no-hit the Braves on 4/7/79, 6-0. His was the earliest no-hitter ever. Bob Feller threw one on opening day in 1940 but it was on April 16th. Bob Forsch pitched his second no-hitter on 9/26/83 against Montreal.

832. Paul (.333) and Lloyd Waner (.316), and Bob (.309) and Emil Meusel (.310).

833. Lloyd and Paul Waner, Pittsburgh, 9/14/38.

834. Alex Johnson.

835.

Jim Bagby, Sr.	Cleveland	1920
Jim Bagby, Jr.	Boston Red Sox	1946
Dolph Camilli	Brooklyn	1941
Doug Camilli	Los Angeles	1963
Jim Hegan	Cleveland	1948, 1954
Mike Hegan	Oakland	1972
Ray Boone	Cleveland	1948
Bob Boone	Philadelphia	1980.

836. Dale Berra, NY Yankee infielder, and his brother Tim, former Baltimore Colt wide receiver, are both sons of Yankee great Yogi Berra.

837. Cuccinello.

Questions

838. What brothers shut out the opposition in both ends of a doubleheader?

839. What 2nd baseman had a brother who played for Green Bay of the NFL?

840. Who was the only player to have as many as two sons in the bigs?

841. What father/son combination came closest to playing in the same season?

Answers

838. St. Louis Cardinal aces Dizzy and Paul Dean blanked Brooklyn on 9/21/34.

839. New York Yankee Willie Randolph, whose brother Terry was an NFL cornerback.

840. George Sisler. His two big league sons were Dave and Dick.

841. Jim and Mike Hegan. Father Jim ended his career in 1960 with the Cubs, while son Mike began his career with the Yankees in 1964.

Questions

IRON MEN

842. What two men share the record for playing the most seasons with the same club?

843. Who are the two players to perform in over 500 consecutive games twice?

844. Who were the only three players active in the 1930s, 1940s, 1950s, and 1960s?

845. Who were the only three players active in the 1950s, 1960s, 1970s, and 1980s?

846. What pitcher holds the record for having won two complete games in one day most often?

847. Who holds the lifetime record for innings pitched?

848. What pitcher appeared in the most games in his career?

849. Who was the last pitcher to start a doubleheader?

850. What team holds the record for complete games by its pitching staff in one season?

Answers

IRON MEN

842. Baltimore's Brooks Robinson and Boston's Carl Yastrzemski each spent their entire 23-year careers with the same club.

843. Charley Gehringer, 1928-31 and 1932-35, and Pete Rose, 1973-77, and 1978-81.

844. Mickey Vernon, Ted Williams, and Early Wynn.

845. Jim Kaat, Tim McCarver, and Willie McCovey.

846. Joe McGinnity earned his moniker of "Iron Man" with the New York Giants in 1903 when he won complete game doubleheaders *three* times.

847. Cy Young, 7,377.

848. Hoyt Wilhelm, 1,070. Roy Face holds the record for appearances in one league (NL) with 846.

849. Wilbur Wood, 7/20/73, Chicago (AL), vs. New York. However, the Yanks swept the White Sox.

850. The record for a 154-game schedule was set by the 1904 Boston Red Sox who completed 148 of 157 games with only *five* pitchers! The 162-game record is held by the 1980 Oakland A's with 94.

Questions

851. Who are the only two men to play in five decades in the majors?

852. Who holds the record for games pitched by a left-hander?

853. What pitcher played the most seasons in the majors?

854. What player holds the record for the most consecutive seasons with 600 or more at bats?

855. What pitcher holds the record for complete games in a season?

856. Who was the last pitcher to win both games of a doubleheader?

857. What pitcher hurled the most innings in one season?

858. What pitcher hurled more years in the same league than anyone else?

859. What team took part in the most consecutive doubleheaders?

Answers

851. Minnie Minoso appeared in his fifth decade when he pinch-hit for the Chicago White Sox on 10/5/80. The 57-year-old popped up. Minoso started his career in 1949 with Cleveland and later played for the White Sox, Senators, and Cardinals. The only other player to appear in five decades was Nick Altrock, who began with Louisville in 1898 and moved over to the American League to play with Boston, Chicago, and Washington. His last game was in 1933 at the age of 56.

852. Sparky Lyle, 899.

853. Jim Kaat, 25, 1959-83.

854. Pete Rose, 13, 1968-80.

855. William White completed 74 of his 75 starts for Cincinnati in 1879.

856. Emil Levsen, Cleveland, 8/28/26.

857. William White, Cincinnati, 683 innings in 1879.

858. Early Wynn played his entire 23-year career in the American League.

859. The Boston Braves, 9, from 9/4/28 through 9/15/28.

Questions

860. *By innings, what was the longest game ever played?*

861. *By the clock, what was the longest game ever played?*

862. *What player appeared in the most games in one season?*

863. *Who holds the NL record for playing in the most consecutive games?*

Answers

860. The Boston Braves and the Brooklyn Dodgers played a 26-inning, 1-1 tie on 5/1/20.

861. Chicago's 7-6 victory over Milwaukee lasted 5:29 (17 innings) on 5/8/84 before being suspended by AL curfew and 2:37 (8 innings) on 5/9/84 when Harold Baines homered into the center field bull pen with one out in the bottom of the 25th inning. The total elapsed time was 8:06.

862. Maury Wills, 165, Los Angeles, 1962.

863. Steve Garvey played in 1,207 consecutive games before dislocating his thumb sliding into home plate on 7/29/83 as a member of the San Diego Padres.

Questions

864. What two pitchers combined to stop Joe Di-Maggio's 56-game hitting streak?

865. What pitcher gave up Joe DiMaggio's first hit in his 56-game hitting streak?

Answers

STREAKING

864. Al Smith and Jim Bagby, Jr. of the Cleveland Indians. Smith, as the starting pitcher, retired the Yankee Clipper the first two trips to the plate on hard shots to Tribe 3rd baseman Kenny Keltner. Keltner made sensational stops and recovered both times to throw out the hustling DiMaggio. Smith walked Joe on another at bat. Bagby was the actual show stopper. He threw three fastballs. Two were outside the strike zone, the third was a strikê. The fourth pitch was a low fastball, and DiMaggio hit it toward short. As the ball got to Lou Boudreau, it hit an object and bounced up for Lou to make a quick toss to Ray Mack at 2nd base for the force. Mack's live arm doubled up Joltin' Joe at first. The streak began on 5/15/41 and ended on 7/7/41. During the streak his batting average was .408. DiMaggio then continued his onslaught for 18 more games. A Dartmouth mathematician calculated the streak will stand until the year 3000. This was not the first lengthy batting skein for the great Yankee. He also had a 61-game hitting streak while he was with the Pacific Coast League San Francisco Seals in 1933.

865. Edgar Smith, Chicago White Sox, 5/15/41.

Questions

866. What two players share the record for consecutive base hits?

867. What club holds the record for consecutive wins?

868. What Brooklyn Dodger went hitless in 21 trips to the plate in the 1952 World Series?

869. What two pitchers share the record for consecutive wins in a season?

870. What player holds the record for consecutive games with at least one RBI?

871. What NL team won the pennant with a 21-game winning streak?

872. What pitcher toiled the most consecutive innings without walking a batter?

873. Who is second to Lou Gehrig's iron man record playing streak of 2,130 games?

Answers

866. Frank "Pinky" Higgins had 12 straight hits for the Boston Red Sox from 6/19/38 through 6/21/38. Walt Dropo of Detroit hit his 12 in only three games, 7/14/52 and 7/15/52. Higgins had two walks in the four games of his streak.

867. The 1916 New York Giants won 26 in a row. The streak also included a record 17 straight on the road. Alas, they finished fourth.

868. Gil Hodges. This frustration prompted a Brooklyn clergyman to pray for Gil from the pulpit in the midst of the streak.

869. Tim Keefe won 19 in a row for the 1888 NY Giants. Rube Marquard won 19 straight for the Giants in 1912. Marquard's streak began at the start of the season, thus establishing another record.

870. Oscar Grimes, Chicago Cubs, 17 games, dating from 6/27/22 to 7/23/22. He was injured on July 7 and out of the lineup for 10 days before resuming his tear. Grimes finished the streak with 27 RBIs.

871. The 1935 Chicago Cubs.

872. Bill Fischer tossed 84$\frac{1}{3}$ consecutive walkless innings for Kansas City in 1962.

873. Everett Scott, shortstop with the AL Boston and New York clubs, 1,307 games, from 1916 through 1925.

Questions

874. Who holds the record for scoring at least one run in the most consecutive games?

875. What team holds the record for consecutive games played without being shut out?

876. Who holds the record for reaching base safely in consecutive plate appearances?

877. What NY 1st basemen played at either end of Lou Gehrig's playing streak?

878. What club holds the record for the longest winning streak at the start of the season?

879. What pitcher won a record 24 straight games?

880. Who holds the record for consecutive ERA titles?

881. Who were the pitchers who stopped the 44-game hitting streaks of Wee Willie Keeler and Pete Rose?

882. What two players have the most hitting streaks of 20 or more games?

Answers

874. Billy Hamilton, 24 games (35 runs), Philadelphia, 7/6/1894 through 8/2/1894.

875. From the time Wilcy Moore of Boston shut them out on 8/2/31 until Philly's Lefty Grove blanked them on 8/3/33, the New York Yankees scored in 308 consecutive games. This streak was the equivalent of *two full seasons!*

876. Ted Williams, Boston (AL), 1957, 16 straight plate appearances. The streak included 10 walks and 6 hits.

877. From 6/1/25 when he replaced Wally Pipp until Babe Dahlgren entered the Yankee lineup on 5/2/39, Lou Gehrig played in 2,130 consecutive games for New York. In only three of those games was the Iron Horse not at 1st base.

878. Joe Torre's Atlanta Braves won their first 13 ball games in 1982.

879. NY Giant ace "King Carl" Hubbell won his last 16 outings in 1936 and his first 8 decisions in 1937.

880. Sandy Koufax won 5 straight ERA titles for Los Angeles from 1962 to 1966.

881. Frank Killen, Pittsburgh, stopped Keeler's streak on 6/18/1897 while Atlanta pitchers Larry McWilliams and Gene Garber stopped Rose on 7/31/78.

882. Pete Rose and Ty Cobb, 7 each.

Questions

PEACH FUZZ AND GRAYBEARDS

883. Who was the youngest player to get a base hit?

884. Who was the youngest man to be inducted into the Hall of Fame?

885. Who was the oldest player to don the "tools of ignorance"?

886. Who was the oldest pitcher to hurl a shutout?

887. Who was the youngest pitcher to throw a shut-out in World Series play?

888. Who is the oldest player to ink a million dollar free-agent contract?

889. Who was the oldest pitcher to win 20 games?

890. Who ruined Luis Tiant's 1968 bid for a no-hitter with his last major league hit?

891. Who was the oldest player to win a batting crown?

892. Who was the youngest player to win a batting crown?

Answers

PEACH FUZZ AND GRAYBEARDS

883. Tommy Brown, Brooklyn, 1944, at the age of 16.

884. Sandy Koufax, age 36 in 1972.

885. This distinction belongs to Jim O'Rourke, NY Giants, 1904, at the age of 52. He caught the entire game for manager John McGraw, in answer to his own request.

886. Phil Niekro, 46 years, 6 months, 5 days, for the Yankees in a whitewash of Toronto, 10/6/85. The win was also Niekro's 300th career triumph.

887. Jim Palmer, Baltimore, blanked the Los Angeles Dodgers 6-0 on 10/6/66 at the age of 20 years, 11 months, 22 days.

888. Pete Rose, age 41, with Montreal in 1983.

889. Warren Spahn won 23 (lost 7) with the 1963 Milwaukee Braves at age 42.

890. Mickey Mantle.

891. Ted Williams hit .328 for Boston in 1958 at the age of 39. He also won the title the year before with a .388 average!

892. Al Kaline hit .340 for Detroit in 1955 at the age of 20.

Questions

893. *Who was the oldest pitcher to steal a base?*

894. *Who was the youngest man to manage in the major leagues?*

895. *Who was the youngest player to hit 100 home runs in his career?*

896. *Who is the only man to win batting crowns in his first two seasons?*

897. *Who was the oldest pitcher to hurl a no-hitter?*

898. *Who was the youngest pitcher to win the Cy Young Award?*

899. *Who was the oldest man to play major league baseball?*

900. *What Hall of Famer hit a homer at the age of 75?*

Answers

893. Jim Kaat, age 42, for St. Louis in 1980, the oldest pitcher to do so since Cy Young in 1909.

894. Roger Peckinpaugh was 23 when he managed the last 17 games for the Yankees in 1914.

895. Tony Conigliaro, Boston, hit his 100th home run on 7/23/67 off Cleveland's John O'Donoghue at the age of 22.

896. Tony Oliva, Minnesota, 1964 (.323) and 1965 (.321).

897. Boston's Cy Young no-hit the Yankees on 6/30/08 at the tender age of 41.

898. Dwight Gooden was 20 years and 11 months old when he won the NL Cy Young Award for New York in 1985.

899. Satchel Paige, 59, Kansas City, 1965.

900. Luke Appling. "Old Aches and Pains" planted Warren Spahn's second delivery over the 275-foot left field fence at Washington's RFK Stadium on 7/19/82. The occasion was the 1st Annual Cracker Jack Classic. Spahn's fastball was clocked at 60 MPH at age 61!

Questions

901. What team was known as the "Wheeze Kids"?

902. Who had the highest batting average for a player aged 40 or over?

903. Who were the only two men to play under seven Presidential administrations?

904. Who is the oldest player to hit 40 homers in a season?

Answers

901. The 1983 Philadelphia Phillies. The players who surrounded 24-year-old starting pitcher Charlie Hudson in the 5th game of the 1983 World Series averaged 35 years, 6 months in age. Their roster throughout the season also included pitchers Ron Reed (40), Tug McGraw (39), Steve Carlton (38), and outfielder Bill Robinson (39). That 5th-game lineup was (with ages):

1.	2B	Joe Morgan	(40)	6.	CF	Garry Maddox	(34)
2.	RF	Pete Rose	(42)	7.	C	Bo Diaz	(30)
3.	3B	Mike Schmidt	(34)	8.	SS	Ivan DeJesus	(30)
4.	1B	Tony Perez	(41)	9.	P	Charlie Hudson	(24).
5.	LF	Gary Matthews	(33)				

902. Cap Anson hit .395 for Chicago in 1894 at the age of 42.

903. Cap Anson, 1875-97, and Jim Kaat, 1959-83.

904. Darrell Evans clubbed 40 homers for Detroit in 1985 at the age of 38.

Questions

BALL FOUR

905. Who was the first player to be intentionally walked with the bases loaded?

906. What Pirate pitcher walked a batter he never faced!?

907. Who is the only pitcher to issue an intentional walk by throwing four balls to the first baseman?

908. What player walked the most times in one season?

909. What two players walked the most times in a nine-inning game?

Answers

BALL FOUR

905. Nap Lajoie, Philadelphia A's, 5/23/01, ninth inning.

906. Dock Ellis had a count of 2 balls on Atlanta's Sonny Jackson. At this point, Ellis was replaced by Ramon Hernandez. Jackson was lifted for pinch-hitter Dick Dietz. Hernandez threw 2 balls to Dietz. Ellis, by the rules of scoring was charged with the free pass to Dietz.

907. Bill Hubbell, Philadelphia Phils. Umpire Bill Klem instructed him that there was no rule against this procedure. A few weeks after this, Hubbell tried the same stunt but was threatened with suspension by NL president John Heydler who refused this procedure for "making a travesty of the game." Heydler was instrumental in having the rule changed in 1926, compelling a pitcher to throw four balls to the catcher in order to intentionally walk a batsman.

908. Babe Ruth walked 170 times for the Yankees in 1923.

909. Jimmie Foxx, Boston (AL), 6/16/38, and Walter Milmot, Chicago (NL), 8/22/1891, each walked six times in one game.

Questions

910. What pitcher issued the most bases on balls during his career?

911. What is the record for most walks in one nine-inning game by both clubs?

912. What pitcher walked the most batters in a season?

Answers

910. Nolan Ryan, 2,186, as of 1/1/86.

911. Thirty. Detroit (18) vs. Philadelphia (12), 5/9/16.

912. Amos Rusie walked 276 batters for New York in 1890.

Questions

WAR PAINT

913. *What Indian lineage does Johnny Bench possess?*

914. *What was the Indian lineage of Hall of Fame pitcher Chief Bender?*

915. *What major league manager, who was himself part Indian, went into Indian war dances complete with war whoops and hollers from his coaching box at 3rd base?*

916. *Who took over for these superstars when they marched off to World War II?*

    Joe DiMaggio
    Bill Dickey
    Bob Feller
    Ted Williams

917. *Who replaced Ted Williams during the Korean War?*

918. *What full-blooded Cherokee who pitched for the Phillies and Cubs was headlined as a millionaire oil baron?*

919. *Who was the only major league player to see duty in both World Wars?*

Answers

WAR PAINT

913. Choctaw.

914. Chippewa.

915. Hughie Jennings.

916. Johnny Lindell
     Mike Garbark
     Chubby Dean
     Leon Culberson.

917. Hoot Evers.

918. Ben Tincup. He played 5 years in the majors, and spent a total of 40 years in organized ball as a Pirate scout, an umpire, and a major league coach.

919. Hank Gowdy.

Questions

JUNIOR AND SENIOR

920. *Who are the only two players to catch a no-hitter in both leagues?*

921. *What four pitchers had 20-win seasons split between the NL and AL?*

922. *Who is the only player to win the MVP award in both leagues?*

923. *Who is the only pitcher to win the Cy Young Award in both leagues?*

924. *Who is the only pitcher to strike out the side on nine pitches in both leagues?*

925. *Who is the only major leaguer to hit for the cycle in both leagues?*

Answers

JUNIOR AND SENIOR

920. Jeff Torborg caught Dodger Sandy Koufax on 9/9/65 (perfect game). He also caught Dodger Bill Singer on 7/20/70. His AL no-hitter was thrown by the Angels' Nolan Ryan on 5/15/73. Gus Triandos did it first when he caught Oriole pitcher Hoyt Wilhelm on 9/20/58 and Phillie hurler Jim Bunning (perfect game) on 6/21/64.

921.

Joe McGinnity	1902 Baltimore (AL)	New York (NL)
Pat Flaherty	1904 Chicago (AL)	Pittsburgh (NL)
Hank Borowy	1945 New York (AL)	Chicago (NL)
Rick Sutcliffe	1984 Cleveland (AL)	Chicago (NL).

922. Frank Robinson, Cincinnati (NL) in 1961 and Baltimore (AL) in 1966.

923. Gaylord Perry, 1972 Cleveland (AL) and 1978 San Diego (NL).

924. Nolan Ryan. He did it with the New York Mets on 4/19/68, striking out Claude Osteen, Wes Parker, and Zoilo Versalles of Los Angeles in his debut as a starter at Shea Stadium. As a member of California (AL), he fanned Boston's Carlton Fisk, Bob Burda, and Juan Beniquez on 7/9/72.

925. Bob Watson, Houston (NL), 6/24/77, and Boston (AL), 9/15/79.

Questions

926. What twelve players have hit 30 or more homers in both leagues?

927. What two pitchers lost over 100 games in both leagues?

928. Who were the four players to hit home runs in each league during the World Series?

929. Who is the only man to win batting titles in both leagues?

930. Who is the only man to lead both leagues in home runs?

931. Who are the only three pitchers to win 100 or more games in each league?

932. Who is the only player to smack 40 homers in a season in both leagues?

Answers

926.

Dick Stuart	1961 Pittsburgh (NL)	1963 Boston (AL)
Frank Robinson	1956 Cincinnati (NL)	1966 Baltimore (AL)
Frank Howard	1962 Los Angeles (NL)	1967 Washington (AL)
Richie Allen	1966 Philadelphia (NL)	1972 Chicago (AL)
Bobby Bonds	1969 San Francisco (NL)	1975 New York (AL)
Reggie Smith	1971 Boston (AL)	1977 Los Angeles (NL)
Jeff Burroughs	1973 Texas (AL)	1977 Atlanta (NL)
Dave Winfield	1979 San Diego (NL)	1982 New York (AL)
Jason Thompson	1977 Detroit (AL)	1982 Pittsburgh (NL)
Greg Luzinski	1975 Philadelphia (NL)	1983 Chicago (AL)
Dave Kingman	1975 New York (NL)	1984 Oakland (AL)
Darrell Evans	1973 Atlanta (NL)	1985 Detroit (AL).

(Listed are the first teams in each league the feat was performed for.)

927. Cy Young and Gaylord Perry.

928.

Enos Slaughter	1942 St. Louis (NL)	1956 New York (AL)
Bill Skowron	1955 New York (AL)	1963 Los Angeles (NL)
Frank Robinson	1961 Cincinnati (NL)	1966 Baltimore (AL)
Roger Maris	1960 New York (AL)	1967 St. Louis (NL).

(Listed are the first years in each league the feat was performed for.)

929. Ed Delahanty, Philadelphia (NL), .408, 1899, and Washington (AL), .376, 1902.

930. Sam Crawford, Cincinnati (NL), 16, 1901, and Detroit (AL), 7, 1908.

931. Cy Young, Gaylord Perry, and Jim Bunning. Milt Pappas fell one NL win short of joining this group.

932. Darrell Evans. He clouted 41 homers for Atlanta (NL) in 1973 and 40 for Detroit (AL) in 1985.

Questions

TAKE A BOW, MR. DOUBLEDAY

933. *What is the most valuable baseball card in existence?*

934. *Who was the first player to earn over $100,000 a year* via contract?

935. *What is the official weight of a major league base?*

936. *Who was the first player picked in the free agent draft?*

937. *What was the name of the first Japanese big leaguer?*

938. *What Hall of Famer averaged .360, 53 home runs, and 166 runs batted in over two seasons only to be rewarded by a pay cut?*

939. *Who were the Giant base runners when Bobby Thomson struck his pennant-winning home run against Brooklyn in 1951?*

Answers

TAKE A BOW, MR. DOUBLEDAY

933. A 1908 Honus Wagner. It appeared on a cigarette card for Sweet Caporal on sepia paper. Only seven were made. The only one left is valued in excess of $5,000. The cards were printed without Wagner's permission as he did not smoke and objected to the idea. The cards were withdrawn almost immediately.

934. Joe DiMaggio, 1949.

935. Six pounds.

936. Rick Monday, Kansas City Athletics, 1965.

937. Left-handed pitcher Masanori Murakami of the San Francisco Giants, 1964-65.

938. Jimmie Foxx, in 1932-33.

939. Whitey Lockman was on 2nd and Clint Hartung was on 3rd when Ralph Branca, wearing #13, served up the "shot heard 'round the world." Willie Mays watched from the on-deck circle, Lou Jorda was the home plate umpire, and Andy Pafko was the Brooklyn left fielder who watched the ball fall into the Polo Grounds porch.

Questions

940. *What outfielder cradled the American flag in his arms so that radical fans could not burn it?*

941. *Who holds the unofficial record for fouling off pitches in one at bat?*

942. *What pitcher had only one eye?*

943. *What is so unique about the song "Take Me Out to the Ball Game"?*

944. *What was Honus Wagner's peculiar batting ritual?*

945. *Who originated the 7th-inning stretch?*

946. *How did the bull pen get its name?*

Answers

940. Chicago Cub Rick Monday, 4/25/76. He received a standing ovation from the 25,167 fans at Dodger Stadium after he rescued Old Glory from two men attempting to burn the flag in center field.

941. Foul ball statistics are not kept. However, Chicago White Sox shortstop Luke Appling once fouled off 24 pitches served up by the Yankee's Red Ruffing.

942. Hoyt Wilhelm.

943. The work, written in 1908 with music by Albert Von Tilzer and lyrics by Jack Norworth, makes baseball the only sport with a song of its own. Von Tilzer did not see a game until 20 years after he wrote it, and Norworth was not even a fan!

944. He discarded a bat after every 100 hits.

945. President Woodrow Wilson. An avid fan, Wilson arrived late at Griffith Stadium one afternoon. As a matter of fact it was the 7th inning. As the President went to his box seat, the fans rose to honor him. Thus, the custom of rising before the bottom of the 7th inning was born.

946. In the early years of baseball, pitchers took their warm-ups on the side of the field. Usually a "Bull Durham" tobacco sign was to be seen on the fence. Thus, the bull pen.

Questions

947. Who is reputed to be the fastest man ever to play baseball?

948. Who was the famous preacher who played for the Chicago White Sox before turning to the pulpit?

949. Who threw the last legal spitball?

950. Who invented the artificial turf of the Houston Astrodome?

951. Who was the first player to exceed the salary of the President of the United States?

952. What was the first team to go south for spring training?

953. What President started the tradition of throwing out the first ball?

954. What year saw the legal entry of the rosin bag into big league baseball?

955. What is the maximum length permitted for a major league bat?

Answers

947. James Thomas "Cool Papa" Bell. It was said he could circle the sacks in twelve seconds flat. Someone once said that Bell could turn out the lights in his room and get into bed before it got dark!

948. Billy Sunday, 1886.

949. Burleigh Grimes, 1934. The 1920 ruling banned the pitch except for those hurlers using it when the ban was proclaimed. They were permitted to continue throwing the spitter until the end of their careers.

950. Monsanto Corporation. Real grass was planted originally, but it would not grow.

951. Babe Ruth, 1930. His $80,000 salary exceeded the income of President Herbert Hoover. When told of this fact, Ruth tried to justify it by remarking, "Well, I had a better year than he did!"

952. The 1870 Chicago White Stockings went to New Orleans.

953. William Howard Taft, 1910.

954. 1925.

955. Forty-two inches.

Questions

956. When and where was the first opening game of the season played at night?

957. How long was the shortest 9-inning game in big league history?

958. Who is remembered as the father of the farm system?

959. Baseball fans were not always known by that name. What were they originally called?

960. What former American League player made a million dollars in one day?

961. What member of the Hall of Fame was offered the presidency of the Mexican League but declined?

962. What forced the formation of the major leagues?

963. In the 25-inning marathon between the Mets and the Cardinals on 9/11/74, how many baseballs were used?

Answers

956. On April 18, 1950, at St. Louis. The Cardinals defeated Pittsburgh 4-2. The first such game in the AL was held the following year at Philadelphia on April 17. The Senators defeated the Athletics.

957. An NL contest between New York and Philadelphia on 9/28/19 lasted just 51 minutes. The first game of a twin bill, it was won by the Giants, 6-1.

958. Branch Rickey.

959. Kranks.

960. Kansas City Keystone Cop Duke Kenworthy inherited a cool million in 1915. To celebrate, Duke blasted a home run for his Federal League Kansas City franchise that same day.

961. Babe Ruth.

962. The American and National Leagues merged to stop player raids from other leagues.

963. 180.

Questions

964. Who introduced arc lights, season tickets, and field entertainment into major league baseball?

965. What Hall of Famer began his minor league career hitting cross-handed and playing short-stop?

966. Who was the first Cuban to play in the big leagues?

967. Who developed the batting theory of driving the ball back through the box?

968. Who were the only two men to play all nine positions in the same game?

969. He played seven positions and roomed with "Marvelous Marv" Throneberry. He scored the winning run in nine of the first twelve Met victories. He got the last pinch-hit in the Polo Grounds before it was torn down. He was removed for a pinch-hitter in the second inning of the Mets' 23-inning game with San Francisco. He was the first New York Met to hit a grand slam. He was the first Met hero. Who was he?

Answers

964. Larry MacPhail.

965. Hank Aaron, with the Mobile Black Bears in 1951 at the age of 17.

966. Mike Gonzalez, 1912-32. He was followed by Dolf Luque, 1914-35.

967. Ty Cobb.

968. Bert Campaneris did it first on 9/8/65 for Kansas City, followed by Cesar Tovar on 9/22/68 for the Minnesota Twins.

969. Rod Kanehl.

Questions

970. Who was the first player to go through baseball's reentry draft twice?

971. What was the only year that saw major league teams "go north" for spring training?

972. Before the current rage of millionaire players, who was considered the wealthiest player of all time?

973. Who was the first player to use the hollow-ended bat?

974. Who was the first Hall of Famer to use the ultra-thin handled bat?

975. What major league catcher was paid to quit the game?

976. Who was the only ambidextrous President to throw out the first ball in a major league opener?

977. Who are the only two United States Presidents ever "officially" booed at the ballpark?

978. Who was the first graduate of the Little League Baseball system to make it to the big leagues?

Answers

970. Steve Stone. He went from the Cubs to the White Sox after the 1976 season and then went to Baltimore after playing out his option with Chicago in 1978.

971. Travel restrictions brought on by World War II kept the teams above the Mason-Dixon line in 1943.

972. Ty Cobb. His Coca-Cola and Detroit automobile stock plus other investments made his estimated worth $7,000,000. Today that would inflate to $20,000,000 or more.

973. Jose Cardenal.

974. Babe Ruth.

975. Joe Garagiola told the Anheuser-Busch advertising agency, owner of the St. Louis Cardinals, that if they would pay him $1,000 a month, he would quit the game to devote full time to his rising popularity as an after-dinner speaker.

976. Harry Truman.

977. Herbert Hoover and Harry Truman. Hoover was booed during the Great Depression and Truman the day he fired General Douglas MacArthur.

978. Joey Jay, 1953, with Milwaukee.

Questions

979. Who batted with his famous "bottle-shaped" bat?

980. What major league player made a valid offer to buy his own team?

981. Who was the first player in the free agent reentry draft to be selected by the maximum number of teams in the first round?

982. Why did club owner Harry Frazee of the Boston Red Sox sell Babe Ruth to the Yankees in 1920?

983. Who scored baseball's one millionth run?

984. Who was the latest major leaguer to bat right and throw left (non-pitcher)?

985. When and where did the first televised major league game take place?

Answers

979. Heinie Groh.

980. Ed Kranepool, NY Mets, 1979. The Payson family refused his offer.

981. Dave Goltz, Minnesota, 1979. Goltz eventually signed with Los Angeles.

982. To finance a musical play entitled *No, No, Nanette!*

983. Bob Watson, Houston, 5/4/75. Watson scored ahead of Milt May at 12:32 PDT after May's home run. Just a few seconds behind and 2,500 miles away, Cincinnati's Dave Concepcion was rounding 3rd base. In the American League, both Rod Carew and Chris Chambliss were tossed out at home just moments before Watson scored. For his good fortune, Watson received $10,000 and a gold watch. The milestone came 99 years after Wes Fisler of Philadelphia scored the National League's first run ever on 4/23/1876.

984. Rickey Henderson.

985. August 8, 1939, at Ebbets Field for a Brooklyn/Cincinnati doubleheader. Red Barber was the game announcer for NBC.

Questions

986. Who were the four players whose last names are palindromes?

987. Who has the largest collection of major league baseball cards in the world?

988. Before expansion, what was the last club to sign a black player to its roster?

989. What year saw the end of the "dead ball" era?

990. Who invented baseball's box score method?

991. Who was the only man to play an entire season without getting paid in cash?

992. What player won 34 games for the 1912 Red Sox and hit .366 in 1921 as an outfielder with the Indians?

993. Who was the tallest major league player?

994. What members of a major league battery were practicing physicians as well?

995. Who published the first baseball card?

996. When was the only time both members of a major league battery had last names beginning with the letter "Q"?

Answers

986. Truck Hannah, 1918-20
Eddie Kazak, 1948-52
Dick Nen, 1963-70.
Toby Harrah, 1971-

987. The Metropolitan Museum of Art in New York City has nearly 100,000 cards!

988. Boston Red Sox, 1959, with the signing of Pumpsie Green.

989. 1919.

990. Henry Chadwick—a British cricket player!

991. Roger Maris, 1962. His remuneration consisted entirely of Anheuser-Busch stock.

992. Smokey Joe Wood.

993. Johnny Gee, a pitcher from 1939 to 1946. Gee stood 6'9" tall.

994. Pitcher Jim Newton and catcher Mike Powers of the 1909 NY Yankees.

995. Old Judge Cigarettes in 1886.

996. On 4/16/80, the Kansas City Royals had Dan Quisenberry pitching and Jamie Quirk catching.

Questions

997. Who was the last player not to wear a batting helmet?

998. Who was the only pitcher to face both Babe Ruth and Mickey Mantle in a regulation game?

999. Who was the first big leaguer to swing a "Louisville Slugger" bat?

1000. Who are the three Yankees honored on the monuments in center field at Yankee Stadium?

1001. How many major leagues have existed since 1869?

1002. Who were baseball's first six commissioners?

1003. Who converted Babe Ruth from a pitcher to an outfielder?

Answers

997. Bob Montgomery, Boston Red Sox, 1970-79.

998. Al Benton pitched to the Babe while with the Philadelphia A's in 1934 and faced Mantle while with the Red Sox in 1952.

999. Pete "The Old Gladiator" Browning, 1884, as a member of Louisville of the American Association. He had the first one made at the prodding of Bud Hillerich. The first game in which it was used, Browning collected three hits.

1000. Babe Ruth, Lou Gehrig, and Miller Huggins.

1001. Seven. In addition to the NL and AL, there were the Union Association, the Federal League, the American Association, the National Association, and The Players' League.

1002. Judge Kenesaw "Old Mountain" Landis, 1920-44
A. B. "Happy" Chandler, 1945-50
Ford Frick, 1951-64
Gen. William Eckert, 1965-68
Bowie Kuhn, 1969-84
Peter V. Ueberroth, 1984-

1003. Ed Barrow, Boston Red Sox manager, in 1918.

Questions

1004. *What player introduced long hair to the game?*

1005. *Who is acknowledged as the originator of the hit-and-run play?*

1006. *What Yankee outfielder accidentally killed a seagull with a baseball thrown in pregame warm-ups?*

1007. *Finally, we have all heard the old saying, "It's not whether you win or lose, it's how you play the game." That may be so, but for the record, what man in major league baseball history has played for the winning team the most often?*

Answers

1004. Ken Harrelson, AL outfielder, 1963-71. The "Hawk" quit the game to try his hand at professional golf. He then became an announcer of baseball games and in 1985 was named general manager of the Chicago White Sox.

1005. Mike "King" Kelly, 1878-93. His daring baserunning inspired the cheer "Slide, Kelly, slide," which later evolved into a hit song.

1006. Dave Winfield, 8/4/83, in Toronto. In Canada, this is considered cruelty to animals and carries a $500 fine and/or incarceration. Canadian officials exonerated Winfield a few days later.

1007. Pete Rose. His team has won 2,044 regular season (1,612 losses), 22 league championship (11), 17 World Series (17), and 15 All-Star (1) games for a lifetime winning percentage of .561.

Sidelights

FOR NAME, RANK, AND SERIAL NUMBER

Retired Numbers

The following provides a fitting end to "The Book of Numbers." These have been retired:

American League

Baltimore Orioles	#4	Earl Weaver
	#5	Brooks Robinson
	#20	Frank Robinson
	#22	Jim Palmer
Boston Red Sox	#9	Ted Williams
Chicago White Sox	#2	Nellie Fox
	#4	Luke Appling
	#9	Minnie Minoso
Cleveland Indians	#3	Earl Averill
	#5	Lou Boudreau
	#19	Bob Feller
Detroit Tigers	#2	Charlie Gehringer
	#5	Hank Greenberg
	#6	Al Kaline
Milwaukee Brewers	#44	Hank Aaron
Minnesota Twins	#3	Harmon Killebrew
New York Yankees	#3	Babe Ruth
	#4	Lou Gehrig
	#5	Joe DiMaggio
	#7	Mickey Mantle
	#8	Yogi Berra
	#10	Bill Dickey
	#15	Thurman Munson
	#16	Whitey Ford
	#37	Casey Stengel

National League

Atlanta Braves	#21	Warren Spahn
	#35	Phil Niekro
	#41	Eddie Mathews
	#44	Hank Aaron
Chicago Cubs	#14	Ernie Banks
Cincinnati Reds	#1	Fred Hutchinson
Houston Astros	#32	Jim Umbricht
	#40	Don Wilson
Los Angeles Dodgers	#4	Duke Snider
	#19	Jim Gilliam
	#24	Walter Alston
	#32	Sandy Koufax
	#9	Roy Campanella
	#42	Jackie Robinson
	#53	Don Drysdale
New York Mets	#14	Gil Hodges
	#37	Casey Stengel
Philadelphia Phillies	#1	Richie Ashburn
	#36	Robin Roberts
Pittsburgh Pirates	#1	Billy Meyer
	#8	Willie Stargell
	#20	Pie Traynor
	#21	Roberto Clemente
	#40	Danny Murtaugh
St. Louis Cardinals	#6	Stan Musial
	#17	Dizzy Dean
	#20	Lou Brock
	#45	Bob Gibson
San Francisco Giants	#1	Carl Hubbell
	#4	Mel Ott
	#24	Willie Mays
	#27	Juan Marichal

The Champs' Ball

One of the most unique baseballs in existence is in the possession of Si Burick of the *Dayton Daily News*. It contains the autographs of home run champions Babe Ruth, Hank Aaron, and Sadaharu Oh.

Cobb vs. Ruth

Ty Cobb's batting average against Babe Ruth when the Bambino was pitching for the Boston Red Sox was .326. In 46 at bats, Cobb had 15 hits, all singles.

Wet Behind the Ears

The youngest man who ever played major league baseball was Joe Nuxhall, aged 15 years, 10 months, 11 days on 6/10/44. Fortunately for the youthful Cincinnati left-hander, things would be a lot better than they were for him in that debut against St. Louis. As the starting pitcher, Nuxhall lasted just ⅔ of an inning, surrendering 2 singles, walking 5 batters, allowing 5 earned runs, and uncorking a wild pitch. To cap it off, as Joe was leaving the mound, he tripped and fell flat on his face at Crosley Field! Joe's next game wasn't until 1952. In his 16-year career, Nuxhall won 135 and lost 117.

Brothers under the Bat

Of the 280 brother combinations who have graced the majors over the years, 16 of those sibling groups featured three or more brothers. Here is the list of those 16, from eldest to youngest from left to right:

Hank, Richie, & Ron Allen
Felipe, Matty, & Jesus Alou
Cloyd, Ken, & Clete Boyer
John, Walter, & Arthur Clarkson
Jose, Tommy, & Hector Cruz
Ed, Tom, Joe, Jim,
  & Frank Delahanty
Vince, Joe, & Dom DiMaggio

Mike and Marshall (twins),
  & Dave Edwards
Chick, Bud, & Tom Hafey
Hugh, Andy, & Charles High
Mike, Tom, & John Mansell
Mike, Jack, Steve, & Jim O'Neill
Ed, Ted, & Bob Sadowski
Joe, Luke, & Tommy Sewell
Len, John, & Bill Sowders
Harry, George, & Sam Wright

Franchise Players

The following is a list of the eleven players who spent at least 20 years with the same club:

Carl Yastrzemski	23	Boston Red Sox
Brooks Robinson	23	Baltimore Orioles
Cap Anson	22	Chicago Cubs
Mel Ott	22	New York Giants
Al Kaline	22	Detroit Tigers
Walter Johnson	21	Washington Senators
Ted Lyons	21	Chicago White Sox
Willie Stargell	21	Pittsburgh Pirates
Urban "Red" Faber	20	Chicago White Sox
Luke Appling	20	Chicago White Sox
Phil Niekro	20	Milwaukee/Atlanta Braves

The Streakers

These are the six longest hitting streaks in major league history:

1.	Joe DiMaggio	56	1941 New York (AL)
*2.	Pete Rose	44	1978 Cincinnati (NL)
	Wee Willie Keeler	44	1897 Baltimore (AL)
4.	George Sisler	41	1922 St. Louis (AL)
5.	Ty Cobb	40	1911 Detroit (AL)
6.	Tommy Holmes	37	1945 Boston (NL)

Young after His Time

He won 213 games in twenty-two seasons before finishing his big league career with Cincinnati in 1933 at age 50. He led the NL in saves in 1931 and 1932. This spitballer hung up his spikes at age 52 after playing with Johnstown in the Mid-Atlantic League in 1935. Supposedly, that is why he was affectionately known as "Old Jack" Quinn.

---

*The 1978 All-Star Game was held in the midst of Rose's streaks. Rose got a hit in that game but it is not included in the total.

"Oh, Those Bases on Balls"

In a game between Chicago and Kansas City on 4/22/59, the White Sox scored 11 runs in the 7th inning with the aid of only *one* hit! The horror began for the Athletics when Ray Boone led off by reaching 1st base on shortstop Joe DeMaestri's error. Al Smith reached 1st base on 3rd baseman Hal Smith's error. Johnny Callison got the lone base hit of the inning which scored Boone. Smith continued home and Callison took 3rd base on the same play as right fielder Roger Maris misplayed the ball for the A's third miscue of the inning. Luis Aparicio then walked and promptly stole 2nd base. Opposing pitcher Bob Shaw drew a walk to load the bases. At this time, Mark Freeman replaced Tom Gorman with the count 2-0 on Earl Torgeson. Torgeson eventually walked, forcing in Callison. Nellie Fox drew a walk, plating Aparicio. Jim Landis made the first out of the inning by forcing Shaw at home. Sherm Lollar drove in the fifth run with another RBI walk, scoring Torgeson. George Brunet then replaced Freeman and promptly walked Boone and Smith, forcing in Fox and Landis. By now, Kansas City manager Harry Craft must have been contemplating quitting as Brunet hit Callison with a pitch that scored Lollar. Aparicio then drew his second walk of the inning with Boone scoring his second run of the inning and the team's ninth. Shaw struck out for the second out. Bubba Phillips then batted for Torgeson and—you guessed it—walked, scoring Smith for the second time. The eleventh run scored when Fox drew his second walk which scored Lou Skizas, who was pinch-running for Callison. Landis then mercifully ended the inning by making the final out. For the record, 11 runs on one hit, one hit batsman, ten walks, three errors, and three men left on base. Poor Landis made two of the three Chicago outs, with Shaw making the third out. Incidentally, Chicago won 20-6.

Like Father, Like Son

Here are 28 father/son combinations that played major league baseball:

Fathers	Sons
Jim Bagby, Sr.	Jim Bagby, Jr.
Gus Bell	Buddy Bell
Lawrence "Yogi" Berra	Dale Berra
Ray Boone	Bob Boone
Dolph Camilli	Doug Camilli
Tito Francona	Terry Francona
Fran P. Healy	Fran X. Healy
Jim Hegan	Mike Hegan
Julian Javier	Stanley J. Javier
Ernie Johnson	Don Johnson
Bob Kennedy	Terry Kennedy
Marty Keough	Matt Keough
Lew Krausse, Sr.	Lew Krausse, Jr.
Bill Kunkel	Jeff Kunkel
Vernon Law	Vance Law
Thornton Lee	Don Lee
Merrill "Pinky" May	Milt May
Gene Moore, Sr.	Gene Moore, Jr.
Mel J. Queen	Mel D. Queen
George Sisler	Dick Sisler
	Dave Sisler
Bob Skinner	Joel Skinner
Roy Smalley, Sr.	Roy Smalley, Jr.
Dave Stenhouse	Mike Stenhouse
Haywood Sullivan	Marc Sullivan
Billy Sullivan, Sr.	Billy Sullivan, Jr.
Mike Tresh	Tom Tresh
Paul "Dizzy" Trout	Steve "Rainbow" Trout
Maury Wills	Elliot "Bump" Wills

The Sultan of Swat

Among the many records still held by Babe Ruth, here are 15 that remain unbroken:

1. Most runs scored in a season, 177, 1921.
2. Most home runs in a 154-game season, 60, 1927.
3. Most home runs struck in a month by a left-handed batter, 17, September, 1927.
4. Most total bases in a season, 457, 1921.
5. Most walks in a season, 170, 1923.
6. Highest slugging average in one season, .847, 1920.
7. Most home runs on the road in a season, 32, 1927.
8. Highest won-lost percentage of a Hall of Fame pitcher, 93-44 for .679.
9. Most career walks, 2,056.
10. Most hits in a four-game World Series, 10, 1928.
11. Pitched the longest winning World Series game, a 14-inning 2-1 victory for the Boston Red Sox over the Brooklyn Dodgers, 10/9/16.
12. Most games with 2 or more home runs, 72.
13. Largest margin by a home run leader over the runnerup, 35, 1920 and 1921.
14. Most consecutive years leading the league in slugging percentage, 7, 1918-24.
15. Most extra-base hits in a season, 119, 1921. This total included 44 doubles, 16 triples, and 59 home runs.

About the Authors

RICHARD VICKROY, 24, is a graduate from the business economics program of the University of Pittsburgh at Johnstown, Johnstown, PA. His work experience has included radio news and sports broadcasting (at WJNL radio station) in Johnstown; a market analyst position with Market Profiles, Costa Mesa, CA; and sales positions with both ATC and Warner-Amex cable television companies. Mr. Vickroy currently is the vice-president and sales manager of MR Entertainment in Johnstown.

HERBERT RUTH, 59, has been an independent agent for the Paul Revere Insurance Company since 1966. Prior to that, Mr. Ruth was a popular radio and television disc jockey/host for three stations (WJAC, WARD, WCRO) in Johnstown.

Messrs. Vickroy and Ruth met in 1974 when Mr. Ruth hosted a music nostalgia/trivia quiz program (at WCRO radio station) in Johnstown. At Herb's request, Rick became an occasional guest on the weekly program, and the two became good friends. In 1978, Herb asked Rick (then a junior at Bishop McCort High School) to collaborate with him on a baseball trivia manuscript. The slow but sure accumulation of over 1,000 questions and sidelights from newspapers, record books, as well as many other sources, was begun. The manuscript was eventually revised, categorized, and updated and has become the work that you are now holding.